◆

THE
DIAMOND
APPROACH

◆

◆

THE
DIAMOND
APPROACH

AN INTRODUCTION TO THE
TEACHINGS OF A. H. ALMAAS

◆

John Davis

with selections from the writing of A. H. Almaas

SHAMBHALA
BOSTON & LONDON
1999

Shambhala Publications, Inc.
Horticultural Hall
300 Massachusetts Avenue
Boston, Massachusetts 02115
www.shambhala.com

9 8 7 6 5 4 3 2

Printed in the United States of America

⊗ This edition is printed on acid-free paper that meets the American
National Standards Institute Z39.48 Standard.

Distributed in the United States by Random House, Inc.,
and in Canada by Random House of Canada Ltd.

Library of Congress Cataloging-in-Publication Data
Davis, John (John V.)
    The diamond approach: an introduction to the teachings of A. H. Almaas /
John Davis; with selections from the writing of A. H. Almaas.
    —1st ed.
        p. cm.
    Includes bibliographical references and index.
    ISBN 1-57062-406-2 (pbk.)
    1. Spiritual life. 2. Self-realization. 3. Almaas, A. H.
I. Almaas, A. H. II. Title.
BL624.D317 1999 98-55925
291.4'4—dc21   CIP

To the Work and the many struggles that bring us to it.

◆

CONTENTS

◆

FOREWORD

I NEVER INTENDED to create the Diamond Approach. It
emerged and developed under its own intelligence and dynamics. It is true I am the primary person responsible for
presenting it, but I have been more a vehicle and, much of the
time, a guinea pig than one who intentionally developed it.

At the beginning, I had no idea that a particular complete
teaching was unfolding. With an intense interest in the inner
journey of liberation, I was doing all I could to be real and
open to the timeless truths of spirit. I was passionately committed to finding the truth of what a human being is, what
spirit is, and what reality is. It was not easy, and for some time,
not much seemed to be happening. Yet I noticed that at times
when my love of truth became selfless, when I was loving truth
for its own sake and not for any personal gain, my experience
opened up and deepened in ways I did not expect. I thought
that my work was beginning to bear fruit when the first discoveries of soul and spiritual Essence occurred, but it has gone
far beyond that. My experience increasingly became a flow of
discoveries, realizations, and insights, revealing amazing and
unimagined qualities and dimensions of Being. As these dis-

coveries emerged, I found that they were accompanied by precise and detailed knowledge about them. My inner journey became an adventure that was thrilling and, at times, terrifying.

It took me a few years to recognize that this surprising unfoldment and revelation of the mysteries of Being was not only for me personally. The arising of the inner spiritual guidance of Being, and my recognition of it as such, led me at some point to recognize that a wisdom path was unfolding. I came to see that a contemporary teaching appropriate for our times was forming. I began to see that it was spirit itself, the true nature of Being, that was revealing this knowledge and developing this teaching. I became a willing and happy guinea pig, going through the various experiences that Being was revealing in my consciousness. I saw that my accompanying struggles with the barriers were necessary for Being to reveal the knowledge of how Essence is related to egoic experience in a very precise way.

Being has revealed its mysteries in my experience in a way that has profoundly impacted my consciousness and transformed it. The person that I am has steadily become a vehicle, servant, and mouthpiece for the truth that is being revealed as the Diamond Approach. The result is the deepening and expanding realization of my real identity as true nature. This identity is the same ultimate spiritual truth that I humbly and gratefully serve. And the beautiful thing is that this process turned out to be identical with the development of the new teaching of the Diamond Approach.

A few associates and my first students also became guinea pigs for the development of the new teaching. The teaching developed as my own personal needs, and those of my associates and the students I was working with, invoked Being to present the qualities and dimensions that were necessary. The Diamond Approach thus developed as a response to real needs in our contemporary times and not as a theoretical construct or a synthesis of existing teachings.

The author of the present book, Dr. John Davis, is one of the first students who joined this work at its inception. As one of my first committed students, he has witnessed its development and has personally undergone the path of transformation of the Diamond Approach. He writes not only from what he has heard from me but primarily from his own personal experience and understanding of this new path of wisdom. The fact that he is also a psychologist who teaches transpersonal psychology at the college and graduate levels preeminently qualifies him to give a coherent and accessible overview of the Diamond Approach. He has a great deal of experience in teaching and working with students in the Diamond Approach, and it is clear that he puts it to good use in the present book. The result is a very clear, detailed, but simple overview of the Diamond Approach, written by one who knows the subject matter both intellectually and experientially. Dr. Davis has rendered a great service here, both to the Diamond Approach and to the many readers who want a fresh look at the human potential and its spiritual dimensions.

Hameed Ali
Berkeley, California
May 2, 1998

◆

PREFACE

THE DIAMOND APPROACH is a spiritual path based on new insights and timeless wisdom. It has the advantage of recent knowledge about psychological development and spirituality that was not available before. Thus, it provides us with a better understanding of profound, but difficult, spiritual concepts, and it gives us more effective ways to work toward spiritual realization.

Hameed Ali (A. H. Almaas) developed the Diamond Approach and has taught it to small groups of students for more than twenty years. His background includes the study of physics, bioenergetics, depth psychology, and spiritual work. He credits his early teachers and his studies of Sufism, Buddhism, and the Gurdjieff work, among other systems, with helping him to open to the discoveries that led to his understanding. Ali founded the Ridhwan School in 1977 to facilitate his teaching. Until a few years ago, the Diamond Approach was known only by the relatively few students who studied directly with Ali. Now, it is becoming more widely available.

Its two main centers, in California and Colorado, have grown, and there are branches in Seattle, New York, Boston,

Hawaii, Michigan, Montana, Canada, Germany, Australia, and elsewhere. Writing under the pen name of A. H. Almaas, Ali has also described parts of this system in a number of books. Some of these are based on transcriptions of talks given to groups of his students, and others provide detailed explanations of various theoretical and applied aspects of the Diamond Approach, supported by case histories. Almaas's books are listed in the bibliography. (Note: Since Hameed Ali is best known through his books, I use his pen name, Almaas, in the title of this book and when referring to him as an author. Otherwise I generally refer to him as Ali.)

Recently, more people interested in spiritual work and the relationship of psychology to spirituality have recognized its value. Jack Kornfield—a popular Buddhist meditation teacher, psychologist, and writer—dedicated his latest book, *A Path with Heart: A Guide through the Perils and Promises of Spiritual Life,* to Ali. In *The Eye of Spirit,* the well-known writer and theorist Ken Wilber writes, "As of this writing, I myself can recommend the Diamond Approach as probably the most balanced of the widely available spiritual psychologies/therapies." Tony Schwartz, in *What Really Matters: Searching for Wisdom in America,* called it one of the most useful blends of Eastern and Western insight he found in his many encounters with transformative systems and schools. Schwartz went on to recommend Ali's books *Essence* and *Diamond Heart, Book 1,* as among the half-dozen best books to begin exploring a "path of wisdom."

Brant Cortright included Ali's Diamond Approach as one of the main approaches to "transpersonal psychotherapy" (although he acknowledges that it is spiritual work rather than psychotherapy). Cortright places it alongside the work of Ken Wilber, Carl Jung, Stan Grof, and others as being important in the integration of spirituality and psychology. Chapters by Ali have also been included in several anthologies on spirituality and personal growth. Graduate courses on the Diamond Approach are taught at The Naropa Institute in Boulder and the California Institute for Integral Studies in San Francisco, and workshops on the Diamond Approach have been part of Esalen Institute's program for several years.

As more people come to be interested in this method, the need for a brief introduction and summary has become evident. Although personal practice is essential to anyone wishing to really know it, and although the books by Ali describe its philosophy and perspective in great detail, a brief overview introducing the Diamond Approach may support sincere seekers in integrating its various insights.

This book began as notes I was using to teach about the Diamond Approach in my undergraduate and graduate classes. I gradually put them into a form that could be distributed to students. They were reading some of Ali's books and doing exercises to explore their own experience, but they appreciated the overview my notes provided them. Here, I have added material to describe its most important concepts and central methods, and I have supplemented the overview with selections from Ali's writing.

The Introduction gives a flavor of working with the Diamond Approach through my own experiences. Although the rest of the book may be somewhat more abstract, I hope you will get a taste of the personal journey that underlies the concepts. The first two chapters introduce the path and orientation of the Diamond Approach and summarize its central method, Inquiry. The next four chapters present its basic concepts. Soul, space, Essence, and the Theory of Holes are key beginning points for understanding the Diamond Approach. The last three chapters present more advanced material. Two particular qualities of Essence—Personal Essence and Essential Identity—are especially important in the Diamond Approach. They speak to the tricky questions of realizing and integrating our spiritual nature into our lives in the world. The last chapter presents a summary of the advanced teaching on the boundless and egoless dimensions of Being. The Epilogue brings the book back to your journey and to some of the qualities that will support that journey.

This is a very detailed and thorough teaching, and I have had to be selective about what I included. Although this book covers the most central aspects of the Diamond Approach, I have had to leave out others. For example, Ali incorporates the Enneagram into his teaching in several ways. His most recent book, *Facets of Unity: The Enneagram of Holy Ideas,* has significantly expanded the understanding of the Enneagram by showing its connection to Essence and to the Boundless dimensions of Being. He has also provided very detailed and useful descriptions of many states and aspects of Essence that I have chosen not to include here. These are important, but I felt it was equally important to keep the size and scope of this book at a more introductory level.

The Diamond Approach is a whole, and its central features cannot be cleanly or completely separated from one another. The threads that I have teased apart and discussed in separate chapters in this book are really interwoven elements of a larger and infinitely richer tapestry. Thus, we see the same threads turning up in many different contexts within Ali's teaching. The concepts of soul, space, personality, self-image, and Essence, for example, appear in a number of chapters.

Each chapter begins with a brief discussion of an important aspect of the Diamond Approach followed by selections from Ali's writing. These will give you a taste of the Diamond Approach in Ali's original voice and illustrate and expand on the concepts. They may give you a sense of his range, too. Some selections are from talks given to students, which are intended to evoke a certain experiential quality in the students listening to them (for example, the "Swamp Thing" talk in Chapter 3 and some of the excerpts from the Diamond Heart books). Some are carefully detailed conceptual presentations (those from *The Pearl beyond Price* and *The Point of Existence,* for example). Others are personal accounts from Ali's journals describing his own experiences (such as the selection from *Luminous Night's Journey* in Chapter 2).

I have, with Ali's permission, shortened and edited some of these selections. However, he has reviewed them to ensure that they preserve the meaning he originally intended. In several selections, I have deleted comparisons Ali makes between his understanding and a comparable understanding from a spiritual system or psychological theory. I value these kinds of comparisons and honor the wisdom in other spiritual systems. However, in the interest of staying brief and straightforward, I chose to not include very much comparative analysis. I encourage readers to pursue the various books written by Ali (all written under his pen name, A. H. Almaas) in order to get a more accurate and penetrating view.

For those who do not know the Diamond Approach, I hope this book will introduce you to it in a way that is clear and not too complicated. I have assumed that you have a sincere interest and some personal experience with deep psychological growth work or spiritual work. I hope it will enable you to take another step on your journey. I also hope that, if any of the ideas and experiences I describe here are too confusing, they will become clearer along the way.

If you are already involved in a spiritual path, I hope this book will enliven and enrich your study. In many places, it should complement and expand things you already know. In other places, it may challenge you to explore new areas of your own understanding.

For those readers who are already working with the Diamond Approach, I hope this book will support your work. You have probably spent months or years working deeply on material covered in just a few pages here. You may also have encountered these concepts in an order very different from the more linear presentation here. Nevertheless, the overview and descriptions offered here might help give you a sense of the bigger context of your work.

Readers interested in comparative studies of spiritual systems, transpersonal psychologies, and the like should find some help from the Diamond Approach. In particular, it shows the continuity of psychological and spiritual knowledge more clearly and thoroughly than anything available before now.

I would add a caution to all readers. Reading this book is not the same as understanding the Diamond Approach first-hand. It will be useful if it provides clarity about what is already happening in your life and especially if it opens new doors for you. My deepest intention for this book is to offer the Diamond Approach in a way that will facilitate your direct experience of awakening, your development, and the realization of your potential as a human being.

♦

INTRODUCTION

I MET HAMEED ALI in the summer of 1975. At that time, my
life was opening up at a tremendous rate. A few years before, I had won a prestigious fellowship for graduate study
in experimental psychology, and I moved to Boulder for graduate school with my wife and infant son. I was enjoying my
studies, my research, and the intellectual challenge of the fron-
tiers of cognitive psychology. I had also begun to discover an
entirely different dimension of my life through encounter
groups, meditation, hypnosis, biofeedback, and other con-
sciousness-raising techniques. Rock climbing gave me a new
sense of confidence and power in my physical body and, along
with massage and yoga, woke me up to deeper potentials for
body-centered growth. Boulder was a hotbed for the human
potential movement, and I was trying out as much as I could.

Until my last year of college, my inner life had been fairly
narrow—or should I say, shallow. I came from a pretty conventional and sheltered middle-class upbringing. My parents
were mostly loving and supportive, but my emotional life was
restricted. Aside from angry eruptions once in a while, I had
very few strong feelings, positive or negative. Moving to Boul-

der in my early twenties offered many ways to reconnect with myself.

At the same time, I felt a deep dissatisfaction in my life. As I moved from one method to another, I found myself still unfulfilled. Even as I stepped into challenging and growthful situations, I managed to hide in the background, thinking I was invisible (or wishing I were). My mind was pretty adept at shielding me from anything that would truly alter my world and my sense of self. I was accumulating experiences without changing very much. I was drawn to new and more intense experiences, but I kept running into barriers to letting myself be deeply affected.

In my deepest and quietest moments, I was torn. Many of my experiences felt transforming, but something in my core still felt rotten and afraid. I found I was merely fitting these extraordinary experiences into the same old, two-dimensional framework. Almost immediately they would pale and lose their aliveness. They felt dead; I continued to feel stuck and impoverished. Driven to keep filling myself, to keep my sense of aliveness for more than a moment, I was jumping from one training, system, or workshop to another. A haunting sense of deficiency dogged me through all of them.

When a friend told me he had found a new sort of growth work that had impacted him, I was mildly interested. He described it as an emotional housecleaning. This didn't have the same flash appeal as some of the things I'd been involved in, but it still resonated as an important piece for me, so I signed up, not knowing just what I was getting into.

Thus, I found myself in a group of eight participants with two leaders, Hameed Ali and Karen Johnson. The "Process," as they called it, involved three months of very intensive psychological work. I wrote my autobiography from different perspectives, I contacted my repressed rage and pain, I relived many childhood experiences, and I began to make peace between my emotional child and my rational intellect.

Still, I was a tough nut to crack. Although I was doing my best, my intellectualizing defenses were very strong. My mind was constantly trying to "figure this out" the way I had figured out other work. Of course, figuring out meant coping with it, not really understanding it. I was busy trying to look good and trying to impress my teachers, while at the same time I was constantly fitting these experiences into my preexisting categories, keeping myself at an ever-so-slight distance from them. And when that didn't work, I would go to sleep, both literally and figuratively. At the end of the three-month process, I had opened up a great deal, but I felt a familiar touch of disappointment. Some core of my life felt unchanged. I was tempted to move on to the next thing.

Yet there was something different this time. Hameed had caught my attention in a new way. It was not that I found him warm, personable, or charismatic (although surely I have seen his kindness and tenderness since then). He was a direct and often stern guide. I saw his sense of compassion and humor, but mostly it was an undaunted quality that struck me. He had the most steady, unobstructed presence I had ever encountered, before or since. Some part of me responded to him, though he did not fit any of my pictures of the kind of teacher I would be attracted to. I guess I had always expected someone who would combine the warmth I had at times felt with my mother and the approval I wanted from my father. I felt neither of these from Hameed in those first three months, but what I did find was much more rewarding.

When he said that some of those who had completed the Process had formed a small ongoing group and that he was leading it, I signed up. We began meeting every other weekend, Friday night and all day Saturday and Sunday, often an hour's drive away. It was a huge commitment of time and energy. I questioned it often, but I always found myself coming back to it.

My upbringing, my personality style, and my scientific

training had produced in me strong skepticism and an ability to distance myself in the service of a misunderstood "objectivity." I challenged Hameed and his work often. Yet he consistently responded to who I was, not my fears, my shame, or my avoidance. When I tested him by hiding behind concepts, he drew me out, sometimes gently and sometimes with a challenge. When I faded into the background or into the pseudo-safety of my fantasies, he confronted me.

I remember a time after I had been working with him for a year or two when I got mad about something and dumped it on him (unfairly). I was screaming at him at the top of my lungs and pounding on the floor. I was in touch with a deep, deep reservoir of hatred and pain. A little later, I realized I was also testing him to see whether he would reject me for what would have been a shameful outburst in my family. He stayed right with me, unflinching.

It took five years before I found myself trusting this unfoldment. All through that time, Hameed was constant in his unwavering acceptance and presence.

Many of those early years in the Work (as he called it) were aimed at opening up my restricted emotional life. Through the Process and my subsequent work with Hameed, I gained more insight into the underlying dynamics of this pattern. I came to appreciate even more my mother's kindness, generosity, playfulness, and humor. However, I also realized that her kindness was often driven by a deeper guilt and that much of her humor had a cutting edge to it. It seemed that my father was away most of the time, working to provide for his family's material needs. I came to a deeper gratitude for him, and we found new connections. I also came to understand how often he was distant emotionally or on the verge of anger.

There was a pervasive injunction in my family against strong feelings of any kind, including excitement, anger, or love. The feelings that did come out often felt damaging. I often felt an atmosphere of shame and covert hostility, which occasionally erupted into outright fighting. One of the clearest rules I remember as a child came from a story in which one of the characters (Thumper in *Bambi,* as I recall) says, "If you can't say anything nice, don't say anything at all." I believe it was well intentioned, but it made for a lot of quiet times around our dinner table.

When I was two years old, my mother gave birth to twins. My older brother was now twelve, and he was developing his own interests outside the home. With my father gone most of the time, naturally my mother had her hands full. This was a time when I needed steady support to venture out into the world and a soft lap to return to for "emotional refueling." However, I was left alone a good bit of the time, and my mother's lap was usually occupied. I learned it was easier to hide my needs and feelings than to have them overlooked, and I learned to distance myself from my inner life. This defense of distancing and using my mind to compensate for a lack of real contact developed further throughout my life.

As the Work helped me understand these patterns and their origins, they loosened their hold on me. There was more than just my emotional healing going on, though. Looking back, I now realize that I was also developing new capacities and qualities. Both the world and my inner experience took on more color. What I had previously seen in tones of gray became richer and more beautiful. I felt three-dimensional and more alive to myself. I came out of my shell into the world. I was less afraid to let myself be seen, and as a result, I began to see others in new ways, too. I was curious about how other people felt and how they saw the world. I gained a capacity for genuine compassion toward myself and others.

The group with Hameed was growing, and the Diamond Approach was beginning to take shape for me. He brought in a number of insights and practices. For example, he used the Enneagram (an ancient system of insights into personality and human nature derived from Sufi sources, Gurdjieff, and Oscar Ichazo) as a way of looking at the ego and its core beliefs, deficiencies, and idealizations. Aspects of depth psychology revealed the psychodynamic issues that were binding us, and understandings from several of the world's spiritual wisdom traditions helped deepen our capacities for awareness. Sufi stories, Reichian breathwork, and emotional release were all important in our individual and group teaching sessions. Meditation practices still provide an important foundation for all our work.

All of this was applied to our own experiences and unfoldment. I remember Hameed's referring me back again and again to my own experience to examine and understand what he was teaching. He constantly encouraged me, as he did with all of his students, not to take what he said on faith but to check it out for myself in my own experience.

For nearly twenty years, I worked with him in one-to-one Reichian-style breathwork sessions each week or two. For most of that time, we continued to meet as a group every other weekend. (His schedule has changed recently to a longer, less frequent retreat format.) It was a huge commitment of time and energy, and we were covering much ground. During those years, I often had the experience when Hameed finished a particular segment of his teaching that it was the conclusion of the Diamond Approach. "Well," I would think to myself, "that was great. I wonder where I'll go next." Then, as if noticing an overlooked door on my way out of the house, I would sense that there might be a little bit more. I would peek through that new door and discover that what I had thought was the whole house was just the foyer!

We had begun by working on old wounds and personality patterns and studying personality from a new perspective. Then, Hameed introduced a new set of material on what he called Essence. At first, it seemed to me that he must have been making it all up because, in my own experience, I had so little reference to what he was describing. As I continued to explore, however, I began to see and feel what he was talking about. I discovered that although the ideas were new to me, the experiences felt deeply familiar. In some cases, I have had a sense of discovery of what was there in me all along, but hidden. Other times, I have reflected back to see that qualities and capacities have developed that were not there before.

Every few years, Hameed introduces a new facet of the Diamond Approach, and I have to say that most of the time it starts out sounding like science fiction to me. Yet the teachings always come with the encouragement to examine them directly and experientially. Never have they been given as abstract theories or pronouncements to be taken on faith. Each of these facets could be a whole system on its own, but he has shown how they are all intricately interwoven with his previous teaching. Each segment has provided me with a whole new perspective that made all the previous teaching come alive in a new light. Again and again, I had a sense of "Oh, that's what that was all about."

It was many years before I stopped being surprised when what I thought was finished turned out to be just another step. Yet I have never stopped marveling and feeling grateful when what had seemed complete opened into an even greater and more complete context. It was as if the journey were a set of inside-out Chinese boxes. I had started in the smallest and most restrictive, and every time I stepped into a newer, larger one, I felt a great sense of relief and freedom. Instead of finding smaller and smaller boxes inside, I was finding bigger and bigger boxes outside, each more radiant and refined than the one before.

At times, Hameed has encouraged us to explore other avenues of personal and spiritual development along with the Diamond Approach. My own explorations led me to work with wilderness experience as a spiritual practice. For sixteen years, I have participated in and guided wilderness trips that incorporate solitude, fasting, and direct contact with the earth. I value this work enormously and have found over and over that my work with the Diamond Approach and my wilderness work, as a student and a teacher of both, have complemented and expanded each other. Hameed's teaching has allowed me to understand and more deeply take in the lessons of an earth-centered spirituality.

I also found that systems-oriented marriage counseling with a very skillful and insightful therapist helped my own development, as well as my marriage, a lot. I feel that my work with the Diamond Approach has helped me to go deeper with this counseling and to get more value from it. The question of the timing of exploring these other avenues is very important, though. For me, there have been times when looking into other systems was a way to avoid a difficult issue. By avoiding my work with the Diamond Approach, I was unconsciously avoiding a certain wound. At those times, Hameed guided me to stay with what was coming up and not to distract myself. However, Hameed has never presented his work as a closed system.

In his work, Hameed was taking us into a territory, a spiritual landscape, that I couldn't even imagine. I began to realize that the emotional and psychological work was really the doorway—necessary, but only a beginning. With his support and guidance, I began to experience more and more subtle states, states of unconditional peace, strength, self-worth, love, and intimacy with my life. I was experiencing a depth and richness that touched me very deeply. Each new experience brought up deeper defenses, issues, pain, and fear. I came to realize that this was a necessary part of my expansion and development.

I also learned something that seemed so right and obvious in retrospect but that I had never heard before. I don't have to get rid of my ego; my task is to understand it, accept it, and allow it to unfold. (I will say more about this later in the book; for now, I would just point to it as a central feature of

Hameed's teaching.) The irony is that, for so many years, and even now, I have had to work hard to disidentify from my ego's reactions and to free myself from its hold. There was no way around that work. Yet what I have finally understood is that the ego is really only the product of halted development. I have come to an understanding of my stuckness. This brings a compassion for my suffering and an even greater appreciation for these difficulties.

I am learning to walk the line between not indulging in my ego patterns while not rejecting them, either. I can appreciate the unique terrain of my own life. Hameed has held with great caring the gifts, triumphs, tragedies, and accidents that make my life unique. In a way, working with him has been the opposite of cloning. I have come to be more assured of my absolute uniqueness, even while I discover my seamless connection with all that is.

Initially, Hameed didn't spend a lot of time naming and explaining Essential states and their correlated issues. Nor did we do a lot of comparative analysis between systems. This came some years later in his teaching. His focus has always been more on opening up to whatever is happening in the moment. He was interested not only in the experience itself but in the background of our experience, its medium and texture. The important question was, so what? How was I holding onto (or rejecting) my experience? Was it touching me? How was I letting it into my life and living it?

Very early in his work with us, Hameed taught a basic awareness practice of actively sensing our arms and legs, looking, and listening. We practiced sensing, looking, and listening with an open and present-centered awareness. I realized later that this practice, along with understanding our psychological reactions and resistance, is a foundation of his work with us. Although the sensing, looking, and listening practice is a very helpful technique for getting us more in touch with our bodies, senses, and feelings, it is more important than that. It has formed a basis for our work on presence, witnessing, and the deepest dimensions of our experience.

The shift toward the medium of experience undercut my inclination to "collect" experiences and insights. With Hameed's guidance, I found myself not only tracking my experiences but being able to notice my awareness itself. I also noticed a quality of being less reactive and more present. When someone was upset with me, I was better able to be open without needing to hide or get defensive. When I found myself feeling abandoned, I could more easily tease apart my own old reactions from what was happening in the present. My basic core issues didn't change exactly, but my response to them did. I became more able to examine them and not be overpowered by them. I discovered that by following my issues, I was led to a richer and more authentic sense of myself.

I remember, for example, a time after the end of my first marriage and before the beginning of my second when I was grieving the loss of a romantic relationship. For days, I had been feeling betrayed and resentful, going through the same emotions over and over again. I worked on this in a group session with Hameed. First, I felt my anger and hurt, then sank into a deep sadness. I cried hard. This was not just one relationship I had lost, but all of them. I was an adult man losing a lover, a junior high school student feeling rejected by my friends, a humiliated little boy sent off to school before he was ready, a toddler feeling abandoned by his mother and father, and an infant crying alone in his crib with no response. All these losses at once flooded me, and I felt the deep shame of being unlovable. Eventually, though, the crying subsided, and my shame lessened. I felt a relief and a lightness that were new for me.

With Hameed's support and guidance, I stayed with this lightness. It eventually gave way to a sense that I was being showered with luminescent jewels of different kinds, like a rain full of grace. I was touched beyond anything I could have imagined. I felt held in the arms of reality and blessed, well beyond the resolution of my loss. I saw that what I had lost was really an image in my mind of being loved and that what is really here is a genuine love and value that is intrinsic to my own nature. I found a degree of self-acceptance I could not have dreamed of. I knew the universe to be loving and precious, and I knew I was part of it.

That experience kept unfolding over time. Along with similar experiences Hameed later identified as states of Essence, it led to a greater trust and confidence. My issues about being seen and valued were having less of an effect on me. When they did come up, I saw them more clearly, and they changed more quickly. Of course, that was not the last time I will feel rejection and loss. In fact, it seems to me that my subsequent feelings of abandonment have been even deeper and more painful, often seeming as if I were abandoned by everyone— the world, myself, and God. Yet there is an increasing openness to the pain and to the states that follow.

A similar issue arose years later. I was on an advanced training retreat Hameed was conducting for Diamond Approach teachers. My mother had died six months before, and I had been struggling with a decision to leave a job that I loved but that did not support me and my family. I was with my mother during the several weeks before her death and when she died, and I had time to talk to her and make my peace with her leaving. As I sat with her those weeks, I learned more about her pain and suffering. I expressed my sorrow and found deeper love and gratitude for her, and we shared some very tender moments. In the weeks up to her death, I felt her soul transform from feeling like a thick, black, tarry substance to a clear black fluid and then to a luminous, transparent black space. I watched her struggle to let go and finally succeed. In the six months since her death, I felt I had grieved and let go, though I missed her at times.

During this same time, I was coming to a resolution with my decision to change jobs. After looking at my choices, I was clear about the best decision for my family and myself. Still, "clear" and "resolved" are not the same. I became aware of a psychodynamic layer that was involved. It was an old pattern of getting something I loved and then losing it. It reminded me of being in high school as a popular tenth grader with a close group of friends and then moving to a new school with a very different subculture and no friends at all. At a deeper level, it felt like a replay of being two years old and delighting in being the focus of my parents' love and attention, only to lose it to the babies. At its deepest, it was the sense of having been held by an all-fulfilling reality and then being thrown into a world of struggle and aloneness. With all these layers activated, there was a huge amount of loss and anger tied to what might have been a simple career decision.

The psychological loss of my mother when I was two, her death, and my job change all began to overlap and intensify each other. I was clear cognitively, but there was still a more subtle layer of distress and suffering that I could not seem to get to.

Then I went on the retreat with Hameed. He was teaching about an egoless dimension of pure awareness and emptiness. (I will say more about this in Chapter 9.) The retreat had been very good for me. I found a clarity and radiance I had never felt before. One night near the end of the retreat, I got into a very deep layer of pain about my mother's suffering. As if out of the blue, I was swept away with an intense sadness about not being able to help her or take her pain away. On the walk from the meeting hall to my room, I collapsed in tears. By the next morning, I was feeling intense sadness about my own life and the pain caused by trying to hold on to the images of what I wanted.

As I stayed with these experiences, I came to a place that I can only describe as beyond coming and going. I saw that my mother's life had been precious but that what she really was, her true nature and source, was never born and could never die. I still missed the person she was, but the sadness had turned to tenderness and my guilt had unfolded into gratitude.

I also realized, not only as a mental insight or an emotional feeling, but in my bones, that my life, too, was an expression of that same dimension beyond separation, birth, death, or any other concepts. I needed to make my choices about my job, but these choices evaporated in the face of the immensity and clarity of pure awareness. I felt aware of being transparent to Being as it was moving through me. My job choice, and indeed all my choices, were no longer problems to be solved; they were purely the flow of Being through my life. This flow felt empty and as if there were no substance to it, yet it was radiant. All the world and all experience seemed made of pure, clear crystal. I felt the preciousness of our fragility and vulnerability as human beings. I realized there was nowhere else to go except to abide in the present moment. And then the sense of "I" evaporated into the emptiness, and all that was left was pure crystalline awareness.

Lest these experiences sound idealized or romanticized, I remind you that they were preceded by many years of difficult work and study. And they certainly were not one-time resolutions of these issues. There are still times I grieve for my parents, feel angry at them, or try to win their love (although these times are more likely to be measured in minutes than days). My feelings of being abandoned arise in a hundred different ways, and at times, I still feel resentment for my losses. Yet there has been a shift that I notice when I stop my busy-ness and distraction. My experience is less entrenched than it once was, more fluid and open. I find it easier to rest in the grace of each moment, and I experience myself more as an expression of the flow of Being through my life. I am more consistently able to step forward out of my fantasies and fears and into the truth of my life as it is.

Again and again, I have learned that the focus of the Diamond Approach is not only on the experiences of true nature as Being but on the clarity, lucidity, and directness of my experience. For me, the Diamond Approach has been about a quality of my everyday life, not only about remarkable experiences. The remarkable times are richer, clearer, and easier to describe, but they are only the peak experiences. Most of the landscape of my life feels more ordinary, yet precious and rich. As I reflect back over twenty-four years in the Diamond Approach, I notice that I feel more at home in my life and the world. Most of the time, there is a curiosity about my experience and a confidence that I have what I need to live my life to its fullest.

As I sit at my computer typing this, I am aware of a sense of ease that eluded me for many, many years. I hear a bird singing outside my window, the dishwasher running downstairs, my wife's voice as she talks on the phone. I am aware of some of my thought process as I type these words. I feel a tension and concern: Who are you? Will I communicate this to you clearly? Will you understand? As my attention flows through these different perceptions and thoughts, I feel an appreciation, a light sort of gratitude for being here, now. This feeling grows in my chest until it includes all that is flowing through my awareness: birdsong, dishwasher, Judith's voice, my typing, the tension, the appreciation, and the awareness itself. And I feel myself opening more until all of these are part of the same flow and unfoldment. This flow feels personal; it is every bit mine. At the same time, I feel no separation or alienation from the world around me. All of these contents of my awareness feel as if they are just different shapes or textures of the same medium. It is this openness in the flow of consciousness that, to me, is at the very heart of the Diamond Approach.

◆

THE
DIAMOND
APPROACH

◆

◆

CHAPTER 1

THE ORIENTATION OF THE DIAMOND APPROACH

THE AIM OF THE DIAMOND APPROACH is to live fully and deeply. It offers the understanding and the practices to support a life without unnecessary struggle and difficulty, a life characterized by fulfillment and contentment. As with most spiritual systems, the Diamond Approach invites us to live in a way that both reflects and develops wisdom, love, joy, vitality, power, peace, authenticity, passion, curiosity, appreciation, stillness, pleasure, trust, gratitude, and an unrelenting engagement with what is. Furthermore, the Diamond Approach is grounded in the knowledge that these qualities are characteristic of our true and fundamental nature. They are our inherent and undying birthright.

If we let ourselves be open to our feelings in this moment, we begin to recognize a longing for such a way of being. For some of us, the longing feels like an ache or a sadness just below the surface of our usual awareness and concerns, a background so common that we fail to take notice. For others of us, it may feel like a gripping desire to gain and hold on to these qualities, an intense drive in which we set our sights on some distant spiritual paradise. Still others of us may adopt a frustrated resignation in which we devalue these qualities as an impossible or even undesirable fiction. Perhaps the most common response of all is a kind of numbness in which we sleepwalk through our days, not even considering our deeper thirst. We then delude ourselves into believing that crude counterfeits of fulfillment, love, joy, and wisdom are the real thing.

When we are cut off from our natural strength, our energy and passion are less available. The sense of expansive vitality escapes us, and we feel weak. To make up for this, we push too hard or strain to capture that passion. We try to convince the world and ourselves that we are not as weak as we feel. Bitterness or hostility flavors our activities and relationships. We then mistake this fake strength for the real thing, and we are caught on a merry-go-round of proving ourselves. The harder we try to prove our strength, the more we reinforce our weakness.

Instead of an openhearted compassion, curiosity, and willingness to engage suffering without running away, we find a compulsive need to criticize, and then fix, ourselves and others in order to take away their pain and protect ourselves. We mistake false compassion for genuine compassion and wonder why we never feel really healed and whole. And so it goes; we dream of relief and fulfillment but settle for shallow and unsatisfying substitutes for real life.

When we allow ourselves the gift of seeing our deeper nature as one having vitality, aliveness, peace, and trust, we also become aware of the difficulties, blocks, and obstacles to these qualities. Even when we do experience them, it is only rarely and briefly.

For example, you may feel a sense of unconditional compassion for all existence—that is, until someone hurts your feelings. Then compassion is out the window, replaced by your desire to hurt the other. Or you may experience your intrinsic value as an inseparable part of the sacred mystery—that is, as long as you feel seen and loved. Otherwise, your shame and guilt overwhelm you, and you get busy proving yourself or hiding.

I think we all have had strong and deep experiences of some aspects of our spiritual nature, only to lose the experience. We fail to grasp what those aspects mean and what our relationship to them really is. Although we long for a rich, fulfilling life and believe (or at least hope) that this is possible, it usually feels outside our reach. Our daily affairs are colored by mistrust and difficulty, and the barriers to our potential seem so much more real than that potential.

Rather than suggesting we fight against these obstacles to find fulfillment and contentment, the Diamond Approach invites us to understand them from a radically different perspective. In this view, they are not merely barriers; they are doorways, too. Hurt is not simply a block to genuine compassion. It is also the access to compassion. Anger or the desire to inflict hurt is not just a shallow and frustrating substitute for authentic strength. Experienced and understood deeply, it is the key to unlocking the treasure of expansion, capacity, and vitality that is our birthright. Our misunderstandings, reactions, and wounds open the doors to a life that is real. The Diamond Approach shows us the precise relationship between these counterfeit qualities, their attendant difficulties, and the more real aspects of our nature and our potential.

Even with a precise understanding of the connection between psychological issues and the qualities of our intrinsic nature, the work of self-realization takes commitment, courage, and love for the truth. Our beliefs about ourselves and the world constrict our experience and become solidified into fixed (and fixated) patterns of feelings and reactions. These patterns give our lives a defensive or compulsive texture. Even our understanding of self-realization becomes a projection of these images, beliefs, and patterns. Our usual attempts to free ourselves, based on these patterns, only bind us tighter. Given our identification with the obstacles and difficulties, we can scarcely imagine what real wisdom, joy, and contentment might be. The Diamond Approach shows us not only how but *why* the work of fully experiencing our lives is so difficult.

The Diamond Approach brings about a transformation beyond these images, beliefs, and fixated patterns toward our deeper nature. It means penetrating the false images and patterns and grounding our lives in an unrelenting love for our lives as they are: painful, ecstatic, or fulfilled. Spiritual realization is not merely a linear projection of a life based from the past to the future. It requires a new foundation that is grounded in the present. The Diamond Approach provides not only an understanding of this foundation but ways to move toward it that are appropriate and powerful.

Encountering our lives in this moment, as they are, we begin to respond from the perspective of truth, openness, and trust. We relax into difficulties and unavoidable struggles, with an experiential knowledge that we can live our lives fully. We discover we do not need to avoid or fall asleep to our situations. We become present and awake.

Each moment that we are able to experience our lives more fully and with less censorship, we become more open, spontaneous, natural, fluid, and responsive. Our distress unfolds into a confidence and an appreciation that is without judgment or hesitation. There is a joyful curiosity and a generous, unassuming calm at our center. We discover our capacities to be strong as well as still, tender as well as clear, accepting as well as persevering, relaxed as well as fully awake to this moment and its movement. And through it all, we come to abide in a basic trust in the compassionate intelligence of the unfoldment of our lives.

Everyday life becomes the arena for this work. The defensive, constricting patterns are both the locks and the keys to the qualities of our true nature. The present moment is revealed as both the path and the fulfillment. The orientation of the Diamond Approach, then, is toward presence and the expression of fundamental truths in the present moment. This presence offers remarkably complete and effective answers to the fundamental human questions. The questions are, what is the fullest realization of our true nature, and how can we go about realizing it? The answer is presence.

THE DIAMOND APPROACH AS A SPIRITUAL PATH

The Diamond Approach offers a psychologically sophisticated spiritual system. This system includes an understanding and a path for full realization that draws on ancient spiritual wisdom and modern psychological insights. It is both a description of the full potential of human experience and a method for the realization of that potential. Its insights are fundamentally consistent with other approaches to spiritual truth, although it does not attempt to explain other approaches or reduce them to its own terms.

In this view, psychological growth is an aspect of spiritual growth, inseparable from it. Whereas other spiritual paths might focus primarily on physical disciplines (such as yoga or martial arts), devotional practices, prayer, or contemplation, the primary method in the Diamond Approach is exploring and understanding immediate experience. If this exploration is deep enough and sincere enough, it will lead to spiritual awakening, development, and eventually, liberation.

Along the way, we come to a greater understanding, and we work through the blocks to our true nature or Essence. We develop and refine higher capacities. When we experience a block deeply, it leads to that which the block was covering. This brings a painful experience of deficient emptiness, followed by a sense of presence and the direct experience of Essence. These psychological issues stimulate our growth in a way similar to the grain of sand that serves as the seed for a pearl.

Psychological issues are present throughout the spiritual

search. We move through our initial fears, frustrations, and even hopes about what a spiritual search will mean, to the subtle attachments and resistances present in the most sublime spiritual states. These issues, fears, and hopes have long been recognized as contrary to our deeper nature and as obstacles to deeper self-realization. However, these issues are not only barriers; they also guide us toward the truths underlying them. The Diamond Approach provides us with a precise means of understanding and resolving such issues, revealing them as both obstacles and doorways to self-realization.

The goal of the Diamond Approach is the full development and realization of Being expressing itself in and through an individual human life. It posits no particular end state or experience. Its goal is not necessarily love, wisdom, power, will, action, bliss, peace, or emptiness. All of these are intrinsic to human potential and do arise as part of the path of the Diamond Approach. However, none is a specific aim of the Diamond Approach, so we do not stop there. The journey of understanding and truth continues without preconceptions or prejudice. The result is the free unfoldment of a living reality without constrictions or distortions.

THE METHODS OF THE DIAMOND APPROACH

The Diamond Approach uses a broad range of methods. In private sessions with a teacher and in small groups, students of the Diamond Approach explore their feelings, thoughts, and actions. It integrates emotional, cognitive, and intuitive processes, breathwork, and subtle energies, all within a spiritual framework. (The several case studies presented in this book are examples of this way of working.)

There is also a variety of formats for pursuing this path. Students of the Diamond Approach generally do this work in individual sessions with teachers trained and certified by Hameed Ali, who developed the Diamond Approach. Students also meet in small, ongoing groups led by a teacher. Large-group meetings are used to teach, using a combination of lectures, experiential exercises, meditation, and other practices. Ali and other Diamond Approach teachers also conduct longer teaching retreats. Finally, students of the Diamond Approach engage in their own study and application of this material through meditation, reading, and other specific practices.

These methods and formats for learning the Diamond Approach have evolved in response to the needs of students and of the Diamond Approach itself. The variety of forms that the Diamond Approach takes will likely continue to expand.

THE DIAMOND APPROACH AND OTHER SPIRITUAL AND PSYCHOLOGICAL SYSTEMS

Enduring spiritual truth arises in different times and places. The Diamond Approach expresses such truth, making it accessible to us in a form suitable to our time and place. Because it has come out of our specific cultural, intellectual, and psychological context, it communicates spiritual wisdom in a way that is uniquely suited to us.

Two aspects of the present time are especially important to this form. First, there is much more communication across cultures and between different spiritual systems. Because we can have firsthand knowledge of many different spiritual traditions, new understandings are possible. Second, we also have available to us new knowledge that was not available before, especially knowledge about psychological development, suffering, and healing. For the first time, psychological and spiritual wisdom are available together. The Diamond Approach incorporates the findings of psychology with integrations of the wisdom of a variety of spiritual traditions.

However, Ali does not merely restate or translate others' spiritual wisdom or combine psychology and spirituality. The Diamond Approach is neither a combination nor a revision of these systems. It is its own system, arising from the needs and opportunities of this particular time and place and through Ali's particular expression.

The Diamond Approach is consistent with a number of psychological and spiritual systems. It is congruent with aspects of the Gurdjieff work, Sufism, Vajrayana and Zen Buddhism, and modern psychodynamic theory. It is consistent with many insights and practices from these spiritual wisdom traditions that are now more widely available. At the same time, it draws from ego psychology, object relations theory, and other psychological systems. I believe the perspective of the Diamond Approach is unique among spiritual systems in its integration of the psychological and spiritual aspects of full human development.

The Diamond Approach extends the earlier spiritual disciplines by providing a more thorough understanding of psychological issues, barriers, and obstacles as they occur throughout the spiritual search. And although it is not a psychology, it has much to offer to the deeper goals of psychology. The case can be made that, throughout its history, psychology has been moving toward a perspective such as this. Psychology has aimed to provide an experientially and intellectually satisfying understanding of being human and to provide a means of realizing human potential. The Diamond Approach moves us a step closer to fulfilling the promise of psychology, especially the transpersonal psychologies, by making psychological knowledge useful in spiritual work.

BEING, ESSENCE, SOUL, AND TRUE NATURE

It might help to give a brief map of the Diamond Approach and introduce its basic concepts here in the first chapter. Most of these terms are described later in the book and in thorough detail in Ali's writings. In the Diamond Approach, the true nature of existence is referred to as *Being*. Being is the fundamental nature of all manifestation; it is the ground and the expression of the exquisite diversity of all that is. Being reveals itself as both diversity and unity. From this ground of Being arise awareness, presence, flow, and emptiness.

The soul is the individual consciousness or medium of experience. It is not a fixed entity (as the concept is sometimes understood) but a pattern flow of consciousness. The soul is shaped and influenced by all experience, and it may be structured by the conditioning of the ego (or personality) or by its true nature, Being. In a sense, it is the soul that makes the journey of awakening from conditioned and constricted patterns to the realization of its true nature.

The true nature of a person, as it arises in the soul, is referred to as *Essence*. Essence is the pure, unconditioned nature of who we are. As the foundation for our everyday experiences as well as our sublime spiritual high points, it is always present, though usually hidden from our consciousness. Essence can be experienced in many different aspects and dimensions. It is not just one big, generic "spirit" but a whole world of qualities that can be discriminated in a precise way. When we first awaken to it, we may be struck or touched by a sense of presence, as if what we experience is real in a way that is beyond our minds. Essence is the truth within the forms and experiences of our lives.

The work of the soul is to open, clarify, and purify itself in order to experience Essence more directly, more completely, and with fewer obscurations or blocks. Essence is then experienced as open, clear, and pure. When this same true nature is recognized as the true nature of everything, it is referred to as Being.

Without direct experience of these phenomena, descriptions of them are merely beliefs or will not make sense at all. A fundamental premise of the Diamond Approach is that these admittedly cryptic descriptions can, in fact, be experientially understood and validated. The point of the Diamond Approach is to help make Being understandable as a lived reality and to deepen and refine our soul's openness to Essence.

When there is direct contact with presence, awareness, emptiness, Essence, and Being, these phenomena are no more mysterious than any other. In fact, that direct contact will be even more clear than our ordinary experience. We realize in our everyday existence, consciousness, actions, and relationships that our true nature is Being.

Personal Dimensions of Being

The Diamond Approach provides a systematic description of the various forms of Being, their particular qualities, their dynamics, and their associated psychological issues. In the personal realm, Being manifests as the ego and Essence. These are personal in the sense that they are experienced as being your own and you can identify with them. It makes sense to say, "This is *my* ego or *my* Essence."

Diamond Dimensions

In another realm, which Ali calls the Diamond dimensions, Being is revealed through its universal qualities. The seven Diamond dimensions are Objective Understanding, Pleasure, Conscience or Action, Knowledge, Love, Will, and Humanness. The attributes and qualities of Being that can be experienced in a personal way are experienced here as universal qualities. Furthermore, they are experienced in an objective and undistorted way. A knowing and understanding arise with the Essential quality, and this understanding is not separate from the experience of Being. Here, I am using *objective* in the sense of something's being known in a nonsubjective, unbiased, and unfiltered way rather than in the sense of making Essence into an object. Our personal histories and concepts of Essence fade into the background in this realm, and the qualities of Being are experienced in a more pure way as more vivid, alive, and real. There is, at the same time, a more objective knowing of these qualities.

For example, in the personal realm, the experience of Essential Love is deeper and more authentic than the usual experience of love based on mental constructs and emotional needs. In the universal realm or Diamond dimensions, love feels present in an unconditional way, pure and clear. The heart feels universal. Furthermore, we not only feel authentic love, we know it in a clear, insightful, and objective way, we find pleasure in it, and we discover that it brings with it the necessary support to manifest it.

Boundless Dimensions

Ali calls a third realm the Boundless dimensions. The five Boundless dimensions have identifiable qualities but are not experienced from the perspective of the individual. In the Boundless dimensions, there is no experiencer separate from the experience, only the unconditional experience of Divine Love, the fullness of presence, clear awareness, the dynamic unfoldment of existence, and the absolute mystery of Being. There is no sense of a boundary within or around these dimensions.

It may help to remember that all these dimensions of Being (personal, universal, and Boundless) are always present, although they are rarely experienced directly. The Diamond Approach offers means for experiencing directly these dimensions of Being as the foundation and source of our lives.

The Unfoldment of Being

Being unfolds and manifests in an orderly way from the absolute mystery beyond human experience into the multitude of forms and objects of the phenomenal world. As it unfolds, it flows through these various dimensions in a progression from those closer to the mystery to those closer to the phenomenal world. Depending on the level from which you are perceiving, reality has very different characteristics. From some dimensions, reality is seen as a unity; from others, it is divided. Duality appears in some dimensions and not others. Consciousness can move through the various levels of Being if it is free and unconstrained. The more consciousness is free, the more it will respond to the call of Being. Being will manifest precisely in the ways that the situation calls for.

As Being flows from the Absolute to its personal and physical dimensions, it becomes expressed or manifest, first as the Boundless dimensions, then by the Diamond dimensions, and then in an individual and personal way. When Being is expressed on this personal level, it is the most accessible and the most easily recognized. (And we should remember that all of these dimensions are present at once and that this linear outline of unfoldment is more metaphoric than literal. This is just a general pattern; our experience is much more fluid.) All dimensions—including the physical, the personal aspects of Essence, and the Boundless dimensions—reflect and express Being. They are not merely barriers to or constrictions of Being. Neither are they constructed through mental concepts or social agreements.

Personality or ego structures, on the other hand, do consist of structures that are extrinsic, mechanical, restrictive, and constructed through our interactions with the world. Yet even these conditioned personality structures are seen by the Diamond Approach to be expressions of presence, love, knowledge, will, fullness, flow, awareness, emptiness, and the absolute mystery, however limited or distorted they are. The understanding that all manifestations, even personality, are manifestations of Being is central to the Diamond Approach. This understanding leads to Ali's insights on the role of the personality in spiritual work and self-realization, and it allows for a much deeper and effective means of spiritual discovery and development. Placing the personality in the context of Being is an important contribution of the Diamond Approach.

Most people start their personal work by working on personality issues, reactions, and blocks. They also have some fleeting experiences of Essence. The path of the Diamond Approach is most often a systematic movement and a deepening of Essence from the realm of personality and personal dimensions of Essence through the Diamond Dimensions to the Boundless, egoless, nondual dimensions. From the point of view of the soul, our experience is one of movement, recovery, discovery, and development. From the point of view of Being, it is always complete and perfect.

In order to help make these ideas clearer, I am including lengthy excerpts from the writing of Hameed Ali (written under the pen name A. H. Almaas). These excerpts are drawn from different books by him and may offer different flavors of the Diamond Approach. Most of all, these excerpts offer this path in Ali's own voice. The sources of the excerpts are listed at the end of the book.

The first passage here is from the Epilogue to his book *Essence.* Here he emphasizes the importance of trusting and following your own experience in doing the work of self-realization.

In the second passage, Ali introduces the Diamond Approach to a group of students who have been working with him for some time. They have been using the practices of the Diamond Approach to explore their everyday lives, concerns, and experiences. This exploration has led them to some degree of release from their issues and to various experiences of Essence, their authentic and unconditional nature. However, until this point, there had been little emphasis on the system, method, and understanding of the Diamond Approach. They were, so to speak, eating a wonderful meal without much knowledge about what the cooks were doing back in the kitchen. Here, Ali steps back from these explorations to provide a glimpse into the kitchen.

The Call, the Path, and the Realization

The desire for freedom, liberation, enlightenment, self-realization, inner development, or whatever it is called is not a response to a call from outside you. It is not that you hear of enlightenment, and then you want to be enlightened. It is not embarking on the journey because others, people you know, are on it. It is not a fad.

It is not a desire for self-improvement. It is not an attempt to be some kind of an ideal model you have in your mind. It is not doing something according to some beliefs and opinions you have picked up someplace, recently or in the far past.

The search is a very personal concern, an intimately personal interest in your situation. It is a response to a call deep within you. The call at the beginning is a vague, almost imperceptible and mysterious flame. It shows itself as a questioning of the disharmony you live in. It is your disharmony, as you experience it. It is your own questioning. And it is your personal yearning.

If you want to be enlightened or realized like somebody else who you heard was able to attain enlightenment, then the search is not yours yet. It is somebody else's, Buddha's or Mohammed's.

The stirring must come from you, from your depths. The questioning must be of your situation, your mind, not of some system that somebody else has set up. You can use the system to help you, but ultimately it is your life, your mind, your quest.

Enlightenment cannot be according to any system. It has to resolve and clarify your own situation. The realization must satisfy and fulfill your heart, not the standards of some system. The liberation must be of you, you personally.

The path is you, your mind and your heart. The call is your call, relevant to your life, and it speaks intimately to you.

The call, the path, and the realization are all a very intimately personal concern. Everything else is not yours, and you cannot use it for yourself or for others. But the complete resolution of your personal situation is yours, and that you can use for others, too.

The quest does not bring about improvement or perfection. It brings about a maturity, a humanity, and a wisdom.

The Diamond Approach to the Work

We call our approach to the Work we do here the Diamond Approach. What do we mean by this? Let's take it word by word. Why do I call it "Diamond"? There are two levels to the meaning of the "Diamond Approach." One of them is the literal meaning, the other metaphorical. The literal meaning is the most difficult to grasp, because understanding it requires an experience of it.

So for now I will talk about the metaphorical meaning. "Diamond Approach" means the method that uses the qualities of the diamond, what I call the diamond perception. The diamond has a kind of precision, and it can cut through hard materials without being destroyed. The approach we use here is focused and precise, like laser surgery. Also, like the diamond, our approach is durable, valuable, precious.

Now, what does "the Work" mean? Understanding what I mean by "the Work" will allow us to understand more exactly what we are doing here.

As far as we know, human beings have always been different from animals in that people suffer a specific kind of pain that other creatures don't. All forms of life suffer sickness, accidents, death. But humans experience, in addition to these things, emotional and mental suffering and anguish. We know that throughout recorded history, human beings have experienced emotional pain, dissatisfaction, a lack of contentment, a lack of peace. What you are experiencing now is nothing new. It has always existed. These days, maybe this kind of suffering is greater or deeper than it was thousands of years ago, but it is still generally the same.

Also, there have always existed a few people with the knowledge that most of this suffering is due to our alienation from ourselves. Most of our dissatisfaction comes not from sickness or material problems, but from not being ourselves. Not much can be done about the suffering caused by sickness or aging. Some people have seen, however, that the emotional suffering is not inevitable in the same way. It is due to not knowing who we are, to not knowing our being, our true nature, not being free to be ourselves. It is this alienation which leaves us with a sense of emptiness, of deep suffering.

Along with this knowledge of the cause of our suffering, there has also existed the knowledge of how to lead a person back to himself, if he or she wants and is able to do it. So "the Work" means any way, or school, or method, which recognizes the fact of suffering and the cause of unnecessary suffering, and works to lead us back to our true nature and thus eliminate the unnecessary suffering which is caused by the split in us.

The purpose of the Work, however, is not primarily to eliminate suffering. The desire to return to one's true nature is an innate impulse, which is there in the presence or even in the absence of suffering. The more we are in touch with ourselves, the more we feel this innate desire to know and to be who we really are. We want the freedom to live as we're supposed to live, to fulfill all our potential. When we don't, we suffer, but that suffering, rather than being a problem that the Work aims to solve, is simply a hunger for our true selves to live, to be free; it is a signal that we want to return to our true nature.

So, the purpose of many schools and methods throughout history has been to bring people back to themselves. This impulse to return to one's true nature has also inspired religions and spiritual movements all over the world.

As you know, these words fail, as words do, to communicate the reality of the glimpses of the Work's value that some of you have had. The Work, we see, is very old; it has existed as long as humanity.

So what, more specifically now, is our approach, the Diamond Approach to the Work? To come closer to an understanding of the Diamond Approach, we can look at the question of the difficulty of the Work.

It has always been assumed by those who are in the Work or who have established schools for the Work, that it is very difficult to actually do the Work and get back to who we are. It

The Diamond Approach

has always been assumed, too, that very few people, only a small part of humanity, will attempt to take the path of returning, and that fewer still will get anywhere, and that even fewer still actually complete the path. We have all heard stories about the barriers and the perils of the Work. The path has been perilous, and because of this, very few have attempted it and very, very few have completed it.

It has always been assumed that it is in the nature of the Work that it is difficult. What we are now learning, however, is that, contrary to the assumptions of the past, it is not in the nature of the Work to be so difficult. The reason it has seemed so up to now is due, amongst other things, to the lack of a certain kind of knowledge, what we call psychological knowledge.

It has been assumed, for instance, that a person needs tremendous will and determination to be able to do the Work.

The task does need tremendous will and determination, and in the past, the failure to use sufficient will has been blamed on the student. The teacher says that the student is not committed enough, not determined enough, doesn't use his or her will enough. And this is true. It has always been and is still the case in the Work. So the teachers push the students, do all kinds of things to get them through—tempt them, push them—whatever will succeed in getting them to use their will, their determination, in order to continue working.

But now we understand that we cannot use our will if the will is being blocked and repressed. And we know that the will gets blocked and repressed for certain specific reasons. Our work in this group has shown us that one of the many causes of the repression of the will is the fear of feeling castrated. This unconscious fear is well known and commonly documented in the psychoanalytic literature, though its connection with the will is generally not seen.

So, the moment we try to use our will, we begin to experience a terrible fear, the fear of castration, be it sexual castration, or the castration of one's self, one's energy, one's will. We don't even know this fear is there. We only know that this will is not available, that we cannot act with determination, cannot do difficult things.

Now, regardless of how you push a person, how are we going to find this will if we feel something terrible is going to happen to us if we get close to it? No matter how convincing the teacher is, we cannot get close to these fears. It's not that we don't want to use our will, it's that we don't know how to, we can't. It's not available to us, due to repression. It has been cut off because of certain specific unconscious fears; and because these fears are unconscious, the conscious mind has no control over them, so when you push against them, they get stronger. It's like rubber—when you push against it, it doesn't give in but pushes back at you.

Or a teacher may tell you to "surrender," and you know that yes, it's the best thing to surrender, but you don't know how to. You're terrified—"What do you mean, surrender?" To the unconscious, surrender means loss, giving up part of yourself, disintegration—terrible things.

It is the developments in psychology which have occurred mainly in the present century that allow us to see how people are stuck in, and controlled by, conditioning from infancy and childhood. The approach of psychology and psychotherapy, which has arisen in the West, is a new approach to the problem of the emotional suffering of humankind. Since the time of Freud, much knowledge has accumulated about the unconscious and about the personality. Psychology, the science of the mind, provides a lot of understanding that has been lacking in the Work. But those people who have developed the knowledge and practice of psychology are not, in general, those who are in the Work. They do recognize the suffering in human nature and work to alleviate it by trying to resolve the conflicts in a person on an emotional level.

As a rule, Essence is not recognized in psychology and psychotherapy. So the alienation from Essence is not seen. It is seen that people are not in touch with their emotions and their sensations. It is seen that people are controlled by complex structures of unconscious beliefs, fears, defenses. But that extra dimension, the existence of the true being, is not generally seen or taken into consideration in psychological theory.

From the perspective of the Work, it is clear that these approaches cannot be completely successful in eliminating the suffering if they don't take into consideration the fact of Essence and of our alienation from it. The most basic cause of our suffering is not emotional conflict. We have emotional conflict because we don't have the knowledge of our true nature.

In psychology, emotional conflicts are seen as the cause of suffering. What is generally not seen is that these conflicts in childhood have the effect of, or take the form of, alienation from the essential parts of ourselves, which are the source of our happiness and joy and fulfillment.

To summarize so far, we see that the effectiveness of [spiritual] Work schools has been limited by a lack of knowledge of the specific unconscious barriers which prevent us from experiencing the corresponding Essential states which make up our true nature. The effectiveness of psychotherapy has been limited by its ignorance of Essential states, so that resolutions occur on the levels of ego and emotions, which are not the levels on which we are ultimately satisfied.

In the past decade, some people have begun to integrate these two approaches, and have had some degree of success, depending on their experience and knowledge. But this is not yet the Diamond Approach to the Work. So far, the attempts at integrating the Work with the knowledge of conditioning and the structure of the unconscious have been very general. It has been effective for some people, but still perpetuates an unnecessary split between students who are still largely identified with their false personality and those students' experience of Essence. So far, the pattern is that the psychological work is expected to take students from point A to point B. Then the Work takes them from point B to point C. Psychological work is undertaken to dissolve the false personality, and only then the possibility for Essential development exists.

The Diamond Approach is different from these approaches in that it works on the perception and dissolution of the false personality simultaneously with the perception and development of Essential states.

So you see, although in the course of doing this Work using the Diamond Approach we accomplish the tasks of psychotherapy, my interest here is not in psychotherapy. My interest is in the Work. Without actually doing the work on Essence, there is no resolution to our suffering, and no opportunity to realize our true nature.

There is no need for us to work just on problems and symptoms here, and there is no need for us to isolate ourselves from the world in a monastery in order to work on Essence. In fact, we need to do this work while we are in the world; it is while we are in relationships, while we're working at our jobs or having trouble with our cars, dealing with money troubles, that we have just the material we need to work with. As we see, using the psychological techniques along with Work methods allows us to accomplish the aim of the Work in an easier, more efficient way than has often been possible in the past. It is necessary to see that our search for understanding and truth is the most important thing here, for these things will eventually lead us to the possibility of experiencing and developing all the aspects of our Essence.

We are learning that it doesn't work to try to develop one aspect of Essence without the others. We're not trying, for instance, to develop love alone. Love is just one of the aspects of Essence. We don't want you just to be loving. If you have love but you have no will, your love will not even be real. Or if you have will but no love, you will be powerful and strong, but without any idea of real humanity, enjoyment, or love. If you have love and will, but no objective consciousness, then your love and your will may be directed toward the wrong things. Your actions will not be exact or appropriate. Only the development of all the qualities will enable us to become full, true human beings.

The Work we do here does require commitment, dedication, and sincerity. We don't require these things absolutely, because we understand that there are barriers to them which must be worked through. Similarly, I don't ask people for absolute obedience or absolute trust. I just ask them to try to understand themselves. Through your own experience, you will discover whether our approach is trustworthy or not, and in time you will see your barriers to trust. There is no need for blind trust; there is no need for blind love; there is no need for anything blind. The Diamond Approach is the seeing, is the understanding itself. So in the beginning, the student needs only sincerity, and the understanding that the barriers to your fulfillment are inside you, and so is the fulfillment itself. What is required from me by the Diamond Approach is the same thing that is required of you. In addition, what is needed from the teacher is the ability to embody the Essential qualities, and, therefore, to be able to perceive them in you. It is required that I perceive your Essence and know what it is I am seeing. But then, the only way you can know about it is tasting it, experiencing it within yourself.

These things are the same as have always been required in the Work. Now we have added the new knowledge of this century, the tremendous knowledge of psychology. I think we're putting it to good use, actually using it the way it is meant to be used. I feel thankful, grateful to the people who have developed this knowledge.

◆

CHAPTER 2

THE METHOD
OF INQUIRY

THE DIAMOND APPROACH aims to deepen our experience of the present moment and expand our potential for authentic fulfillment. It has adapted and integrated many methods, including meditation and awareness practices, Reichian breathwork, and psychological methods of focusing, questioning, interpretation, confrontation, support, and mirroring. It incorporates these methods in individual, small-group, and large-group formats. The books in Ali's Diamond Mind Series include case studies of students working with him and give a flavor of the methods of the Diamond Approach. One is included in this chapter.

Within this eclecticism, the central practice of the Diamond Approach is what Ali calls *Inquiry*. It exemplifies the Diamond Approach's orientation to growth and self-realization and leads to understanding and experiencing in a complete and experiential way. Inquiry is the practice; understanding is the result. Ali uses the term *understanding* in a specific way in the Diamond Approach. This understanding is not merely an intellectual picture. It incorporates intellect, heart, body, and intuition in the pursuit of the truth of our nature. Eventually, understanding becomes a merging of awareness with the dynamic unfoldment of the present. Then, presence and understanding come together, and Inquiry is spontaneous. Ultimately, understanding is the action of Being on the mind. Being reveals itself through the mind as understanding.

This kind of experiencing is antithetical to ego identification, attachment, judgment, defensiveness, and reductionism. It is characterized by joy in the unending discovery of truth and peace in the fullness of Being. It is fueled by strength and determination to experience yourself and your life fully. And it is compassionately open to whatever is to be found, without a trace of rejection, prejudice, or preconception.

Understanding involves being fully present with your immediate experience. It also involves being present with the unfoldment of experience; thus, understanding is dynamic, not static. Understanding requires kindness to yourself, awareness, and dedication to the truth, no matter what the consequences. The Diamond Approach's method of Inquiry leads to this holistic understanding in a way that is open, sincere, discriminating, and genuinely curious.

THE PRACTICE OF INQUIRY

Inquiry encourages and enables open-ended exploration into your immediate experience without preconceptions or prejudice about the outcome of that exploration. Any experience can be the starting point for this search. From here, it proceeds in an integrated way that includes perceptions, memories, insights, emotions, body sensations, intuition, and awareness of subtle energies such as chi. As this exploration proceeds from one experience to another, your awareness opens to deeper levels of experience and, eventually, to Essence. As the Inquiry continues, deeper levels and dimensions of Essence are revealed and integrated. In this way, Inquiry leads to growth, healing, release, and fulfillment. Its ultimate outcome is freedom and the experience of your true nature and full human potential in whatever way it manifests.

Although a "recipe" for the practice of Inquiry is not possible, some guidelines may be helpful. It is always done in the present, as a focused exploration of immediate experience. Thoughts, memories, associations, feelings, and insights may arise into the present moment, but these are approached in the "now." Generally, it is a good idea to avoid explanations or long accounts of previous experiences. Instead, you can track these thoughts and memories in the present. You might, for instance, say to yourself in the course of an Inquiry practice, "Now I am remembering an argument I had last week." You may even describe it briefly, but only as the memory of it is present here and now. You will probably also notice feelings or body sensations triggered by the memory. These are, of course, also arising in the present moment.

The attitude of Inquiry is open-ended and goal-less. It allows experience to unfold in whatever direction it naturally flows. There is no particular end state to achieve. Inquiry calls for the willingness to encounter any sort of experience from the most difficult to the most sublime.

Understanding our tendencies, resistances, preferences, idealizations, beliefs, and patterns is necessary for Inquiry to proceed. Although Inquiry itself helps to provide this understanding, the Diamond Approach employs various models and methods to explore the student's character structure and psychodynamic makeup. The Enneagram of personality types is one useful view that can be used to "jump-start" and catalyze Inquiry. Knowing, for instance, that you tend to get judgmental, distant, or hostile when you begin to touch your inner wounds helps you to recognize and disidentify from them. Then, you have a better chance of understanding them and their unfoldment.

Usually, you hold a particular question or experience as the focus of Inquiry. This focus provides a thread to follow throughout the Inquiry. Inquiry is not free association or mindfulness meditation, although these practices are useful in supporting Inquiry. Instead, you keep this focus and pursue it throughout the practice of the Inquiry. Inquiry includes awareness of body sensations, memories and associations, emotions, thoughts, intuitions, and energetic qualities. It can be helpful in the practice of Inquiry to track which of these dimensions of experience are being used or avoided. For instance, if you find mostly emotions, ask yourself what body sensations, thoughts, or memories go with the emotions. Similarly, if you are primarily aware of thoughts, examine the body sensations, emotions, and texture or energy of the experience.

During the practice of Inquiry, remember to sense your body, breathe, and stay aware of the present moment. It is important to hold your experiences with a compassionate, spacious, and nonjudgmental attitude. The practice of meditation is a strong support for this orientation. For this reason, students of the Diamond Approach are encouraged to practice meditation techniques, including concentration, mindfulness, and certain visualizations, as foundations for the practice of Inquiry.

Inquiry generally leads to a shift in experience. This shift may feel like an insight, a release of energy, a strong (or subtle) emotional state, or a spaciousness in your awareness. However, these kinds of shifts are not its aim, and they are not final. Instead, they may open you to a deeper experience of Essence or to a deeper issue that needs to be understood. This distinguishes Inquiry from apparently similar processes in psychotherapy and many spiritual disciplines. Inquiry is not aimed at any particular behavior change or psychotherapeutic outcome. Nor is its goal to evoke any particular state or spiritual quality.

Initially, Inquiry is done as a specific method, either alone or with others and usually with the guidance of a teacher. Eventually, Inquiry becomes more and more a part of your life, and you understand and digest experiences more deeply as they occur. Healing and growth, whether psychological or spiritual, occur as a natural development of your soul. Inquiry is a tool for guiding, empowering, and supporting this development. At first, Inquiry is a technique, then a practice, and finally a way of being.

Techniques that Support Inquiry

Specific techniques can support Inquiry. One method used in the Diamond Approach is a dyadic process in which one person asks a question repeatedly while the other gives whatever answers come to mind. For example, a student of the Diamond Approach exploring difficulties in experiencing emotions might work with the question, "How do you block your feelings?" or "What's right about blocking your feelings?" By answering this question again and again for twenty minutes, new insights, experiences, or understanding can emerge. This understanding, in turn, is used to continue the more open-ended practice of Inquiry. The student will use the insights garnered from this repeated question to take the Inquiry to a deeper, more revealing level.

Teachers of the Diamond Approach frequently use body-centered therapeutic techniques to open blocked energy flows and emotions during a student's Inquiry. For example, a person experiencing a block in the throat might be instructed to yell as loud as possible several times to open this block. A block in the pelvis might be opened by bouncing the hips on a mattress or stamping vigorously on the ground. To the extent that the practice of Inquiry uncovers these blocks, they can be incorporated into the Inquiry, examined with open-mindedness, and used to lead you to greater self-realization and development.

One of the early difficulties that can arise in these kinds of explorations is the tendency to judge our experiences. We evaluate them in terms of our standards derived, for the most part, from our histories of conditioning, rejection, and the judgments we grew up with. The function of this inner critic or superego was perhaps once useful to us, enabling us to get by in our early life situations, but we often continue to identify with it and let it color our experiences. This restricts our experiences and our potential, causes us unnecessary suffering, and acts as a major impediment to self-exploration. The Diamond Approach offers a view of the superego based both on psychological understanding and on the knowledge of Essence. Defending against this inner critic by developing a sincere understanding of it and challenging it with strength and energy, along with compassion for ourselves, is an important support for the practice of Inquiry.

Another aid to Inquiry is a focused task or question that you may carry for days or even weeks. For example, if you find that you tend to suppress your emotions, you may watch for specific instances of this suppression in your everyday life. If you are working on a tendency to be judgmental and critical, take notice of the specific ways you do this. (Be careful, of course, not to suppress your feelings about suppressing your feelings or to judge yourself for being judgmental.) After several days of this, you can come back to a more focused Inquiry process with greater awareness. You may also take on a task aimed at expanding your awareness and understanding, such as deliberately expressing a feeling three times each day or, in the interest of increasing awareness, deliberately not expressing a feeling three times a day. Bring your curiosity and openness to these tasks. The point of these kinds of exercises (whether they are body-centered therapeutic techniques, behavior-oriented tasks, or cognitive, emotional, or energetic explorations) is to expand the openness and flow of understanding and, specifically, to support Inquiry.

INQUIRY AND ESSENCE

The various Essential qualities and dimensions of Being are closely tied to Inquiry. For example, the Essential aspect of Strength provides the passion and drive to pursue your experience. Essential Will provides support and perseverance. Awareness provides clarity and open-mindedness. Compassion provides healing and openheartedness when dealing with deep and difficult experiences. Essential aspects provide specific foundations for Inquiry.

At the same time, these qualities are freed and recovered through the practice of Inquiry. Along with leading to the experience of more Essential states, Inquiry leads to qualitatively deeper dimensions of Being. For example, exploring your personal issues of hurt in a particular situation may bring out Essential Compassion on a personal level, experienced as tenderness and care. As you continue to inquire, the experience may deepen into the experience of compassion on a more universal level. With further Inquiry, this compassion may lead beyond itself to an unconditional Divine Love and trust, pure presence, or emptiness. None of these deeper experiences negate the sense of compassion; rather, they give a sense of completing it.

INQUIRY AND THE DIAMOND GUIDANCE

The most central aspect needed for Inquiry is the Diamond Guidance. This is the Essential aspect that provides the capacity for discriminating questioning. As we practice Inquiry, many questions and directions are possible. Rather than suggest strategies to use, the Diamond Approach recognizes that Being itself can direct the process of Inquiry. The Diamond Guidance is the quality of Being that does this. It is called Diamond Guidance because it is free of personal bias and personal history. The reference to a diamond suggests the objectivity, clarity, preciousness, and precision of this freedom.

Let's say you are tracking your experience and you find yourself on the verge of tears when you think about an incident from your past. At this point, you might explore the particulars of that incident in more detail, inquiring into how it came about, what caused it to hurt you, what images of yourself were involved. Or you might explore the feeling of the sadness itself, asking what kind of tears are these or feeling the sadness as a body experience. You may not explore the sadness at all, noticing that it goes away quickly and that underneath it is a simple tenderness or a feeling of anger.

Without the operation of the Diamond Guidance, Inquiry tends to be guided by expectations, theories, and past experiences. You might remember a similar tearful feeling that was associated with not being valued or seen accurately. Based on this past experience, you look for the same connection. However, the sadness you are feeling may be related to something very different. You may approach your feeling with a belief that tears are good to feel, and so you are drawn to releasing them. However, this may be a time when letting the feeling develop without a release will lead to new experiences. On the other hand, you may feel that tears are bad and intellectualize them when it would be more helpful simply to let them flow.

When we are completely open to the flow of questions and experiences, we can begin to experience this aspect of Essence directly. Working through the barriers to this aspect frees our capacity to be guided by Essence. These barriers include thinking that we already know, a fixation on or clinging to answers or beliefs from the past, and a fear of the unknown. To be open to Inquiry and the Diamond Guidance means giving up control over our experience, and it means allowing the flow of Being to take us where we need to go. It brings careful and caring discrimination and an elegant kind of perception, at once precise and relaxed.

TEACHERS AND GROUPS

As with most forms of deep psychological and spiritual work, a working relationship with a teacher is helpful or even necessary in practicing Inquiry fully. At first, the teacher tracks the student's unfoldment and provides mirroring, guidance, and support for the student. This guidance and support occur on several levels, both obvious and subtle. Eventually, the student embodies this guidance, and Being becomes the Teacher. The teacher may also manifest the particular qualities the student is working on, providing a direct and supportive influence. Yet from another perspective, the real "teacher" is always Being acting through a human being.

Most students are part of a larger group studying the Diamond Approach. As in other forms of spiritual work, the group supports the individual's work in a number of ways. The group can strengthen an individual's resolve and perseverance during difficult stages of work, and the group setting facilitates the emergence of personality issues that might not emerge so readily in individual or solitary work. Since the orientation of the Diamond Approach is to do the work of spiritual development in the midst of one's life, group work with the support and guidance of a teacher reflects this in-the-world quality of the Diamond Approach.

In the selections that follow, Ali describes understanding (as he uses it in the Diamond Approach) and illustrates many of its dimensions. In the first selection, he shows how understanding has the richness and power to take us on the complete journey of self-realization, finally dissolving itself into the mystery of the unfoldment of a liberated life. The second selection is an account of a student's work session with Ali. This session demonstrates the method of Inquiry and the natural movement from personality issues to Essence. (He uses a pseudonym to protect the student's confidentiality.) The third selection is an excerpt from Ali's journals of his own Inquiry, edited later by him for clarity. It illustrates how Inquiry can be integrated into our everyday lives.

Being and Understanding
The human potential for understanding is both a curse and a possibility for great fulfillment. The elements of the mind—

memory, conceptualization, thinking processes, creation of images, projections into the future, and so forth—become the basic ingredients of our suffering. Ideas and experiences from the past, from early childhood as well as later on, good and bad, form the foundation of your assumptions about who you are. Your mind holds on to these childhood happenings and stores them in its memory. They become the building blocks of what you think you are, and then you're stuck with them.

What understanding gives us is the possibility of actually seeing through this process. Without understanding, you'll just identify with these old self-images and go on believing that you're a person who has such and such a quality, who is weak or dumb, who eats too much or gets taken advantage of, or feels nervous at parties, and so forth, self-image upon self-image. And you'll go on like that for the rest of your life, which is what most people do.

Understanding offers the possibility of seeing that you're taking yourself to be a certain self-image. Then you can start to ask yourself why. A person who has grown up thinking, "I'm a jerk" or "I'm a bitch," now begins to question the idea. "I seem to behave like a jerk, and deep down I think I am, but why?" "When people talk to me I often respond as if I'm a bitch, but why? Why do I still believe it about myself?"

If you use your understanding, you notice that not everyone behaves like a jerk, but you do. If you investigate, if you let yourself be open and curious about it, you'll find out what is happening. You might discover that your father was a jerk, and you liked him and wanted to be like him. What's more, you liked your mother very much and she liked your father, so you figured, "I'll be a jerk like my father, and then they'll both like me." Most of the time, this kind of decision is completely unconscious. You go around being a jerk, even though everyone gives you a hard time about it, because it helps you feel that Mommy and Daddy are always there liking you.

Now, if you use the point of view of understanding, you can

get to the origin of this pattern. "I believe I'm a jerk and continue believing it, because that way my mommy and daddy like me, and I feel lovable." When you see this, you see how that part of the personality was created. You see that it's unnecessary now, in present time, because not everyone who matters to you now likes jerks. Maybe your mother liked your father that way, but not everyone is like that.

Of course, the process of understanding can go deeper. You might wonder, "What's this big deal about people liking me? Why do I want people to like me? I always wanted to be a jerk because I thought then people would like me. Now I discover that they don't necessarily like me that way at all, so I'll immediately try to find a new way to behave so that they will." You decide that the best way to do this is to become self-realized. So, why do you want to be self-realized? Because you want people to like you. You still want people to like you. And if you pursue understanding, you investigate the issue.

If you didn't seek understanding, you'd just go around trying to make people like you, which is what most people do. But if you apply understanding, in time you'll see why you do that, and you'll see not only that it doesn't work, but that it's not necessary for your happiness. It's utterly superfluous and not what you deeply want to pursue. So, this shows us something about the usefulness of understanding.

However, understanding is also something much deeper. We've just seen how it reveals the falsehood, but we have not yet seen how it reveals the truth: understanding reveals what you are not and what you are. You see that you're not actually a jerk. But then you wonder, "What am I if I'm not a jerk? Maybe I'm a good, loving person." Okay, so you become a loving person. Then after a while you begin to investigate yourself again, not according to whether you're a jerky person or a loving person, but in terms of whether you're a person at all. When you begin to investigate self-image at this level, you begin getting closer to the truth. You start seeing that the notion of a person is another idea formulated by the mind. But the idea of a person is not something you learned only from your parents; it's human conditioning.

However, our deepest nature is not that of a person. We can manifest as a person, but at the deepest level, we are something that is the source of the person. When we come to the understanding that reveals the truth rather than the falsehood, then it is functioning more as a process of unfoldment. Then understanding, which has seemed to be the equivalent of looking at something objectively, is no longer separate from the process of unfoldment itself. Seeing one layer of our reality and understanding it is the same thing as that layer coming out, unfolding like a flower opening up. Understanding becomes the same thing as the process of actually living your unfoldment. Because you understand your experience of joy, for instance, you experience yourself as joy. You become light, happy and joyous; you start joking and become bubbly and can't stop laughing. What does understanding mean then? Part of it, which is revealing the falsehood, sees whatever barrier stopped you from being joy. Then you understand what it is to be joy. To understand what it is to be joy means to be joy consciously, means to actually feel it as your very atoms.

At that level, understanding becomes clear, or you begin seeing what it is: Being and awareness of Being at the same time. Being is our true nature, right? Essence is Being. So you're being whatever aspect of Essence is arising, like Joy. There is awareness of that Being, which is different from the way a child perceives. A child doesn't have understanding. A child has Being, but a child isn't conscious of that Being. The child is happy, but doesn't know it, doesn't consciously feel it. Happiness is expressed, but not consciously experienced. You can tell that the child is happy, or the child is contented or peaceful, but the child's mind is not conscious of it.

Understanding, then, includes the mind becoming an expression or a channel for Being. Mind becomes connected to

Being, not separate from it like it was when you were a child, or like it was when you were an adult just seeing your issues. At this level understanding becomes the unity, the interface, the meeting of Being and mind. You are Being, but there is also awareness of the beingness. This consciousness of beingness is understanding.

An Inquiry with a Student

Sandy is a married woman in her thirties who has been working with the author in a group situation. Her explicit reason for being in the group is to understand herself, to grow, and to learn to be more herself. She was sick for some time, and has been back in the group for only a couple of months. She begins speaking, obviously with some guilt about what she is feeling. She relates hesitatingly that she almost did not come to the group meeting this particular evening and has been feeling increasingly unwilling to come to the sessions. When I inquire whether she knows the reasons behind her feelings she says that because she was sick for a long time and did not have fun, now she feels she would rather go out and have fun rather than sitting in group sessions and scrutinizing herself. When I ask what she means by having fun, she grins and says it is doing what she wants to do, and relates that she resents coming to the group because she must abide by a certain schedule and accommodate herself to a structure imposed on her from the outside. So in the group sessions she has been feeling frustrated, hemmed in, and resentful.

I indicate that I agree that it is good for her to have fun and enjoy herself, and that I understand how her illness has curtailed her life. I then inquire about why she feels imposed upon and restricted by coming to the group, when it is her choice to be in the group and benefit from the work done in it. She responds by affirming that it is her choice, that she understands the benefits of participating in the group, and that she does not understand why she feels so frustrated.

As we inquire further into her emotional states, she sees that she feels she is losing something by adhering to a certain structure and schedule: she feels she loses her freedom, and this makes her feel frustrated. She relates then that this pattern is not new for her. She has had the same conflict in almost every job she has had and actually lost some jobs because of it. Even jobs she has liked, she could not completely enjoy because of this conflict. So she leaves what she is doing, even though it is useful to her, in order to avoid feeling this overwhelming sense of frustration and heaviness.

We see here that Sandy is recognizing the present situation as part of a pattern that she has repeated many times in her life, which has brought her much discontent and frustration. As she becomes aware that her reactions to the group structure are repeating this pattern, she becomes more motivated to explore her state. As she continues, she tells me that she knows that this pattern has to do with her relationship to her mother, that she always felt restricted by her, not allowed to live her life as she wants. But she is frustrated, she says, because she has seen this pattern many times, and has understood its genesis for a long time, but there has been no change.

I point out to her that it seems she does not know how to have the freedom she wants except by saying "no" to a situation she feels is restricting. It becomes clear to her that she believes that freedom is gained only by doing what she chooses to do, and many times this means not doing what others want her to do. I point out to her that "freedom" acquired in this way is nothing but a reaction to the situation, and that a reaction is not a free choice, since it is determined by the other and is not a spontaneous response. It is simply a compulsive, automatic reaction.

Here she admits that she does not usually enjoy the freedom she believes she is gaining, but continues feeling frustrated, and, in addition, leaves activities and situations that are actually useful to her. She acknowledges also that even when she believes she is gaining autonomy by removing herself from some situation, she still feels the lack of the true freedom she wants.

At this point I ask her what it is exactly that she wants to experience by having her freedom. She says she just wants to be herself, to be free to be herself. She believes that if she does what she chooses, she will be herself as herself, the way she really is, and not the way others want her to be.

I ask her to tell me more specifically what it means to be herself. In her past work she had often felt that "I don't know what I want," and now she realizes that she has never looked at the situation from the perspective of what it really means to her to be herself. She was wanting something, which she somewhat vaguely associated with autonomy. Now she finds it hard to describe more specifically what she means, and the very asking of the question puts her into deeper contact with herself. Here, I ask what she is feeling now. She says she is much less frustrated, and that she feels okay. I ask her what kind of okay, what does she really feel in her body? She says she feels calm and peaceful, and the issue of autonomy no longer feels significant.

I express surprise that she feels so peaceful, and not concerned about what was such a bothersome issue. I ask her to tell me more about the calm feeling. She says she feels the calmness especially in her belly, and that the calmness also feels strong. The strength somewhat surprises her, because when she was sick she was feeling mostly weak. I keep asking her to pay more attention to the calmness, to describe it more specifically. She feels the strength and calmness growing in her, filling her chest.

I ask her what she means by the feeling filling her. Here she realizes she is not only feeling an emotional state, but that the calmness and strength are effects of a sense of fullness in her body, which was in her belly but now increasingly pervades her body. The more she senses this fullness, the more it expands. The effect is that she feels a fullness of presence that is calm, peaceful, and collected. This makes her happy and contented.

I ask her to recall her desire for autonomy and freedom.

The Diamond Approach

Here, she realizes that now she feels she is being herself. The presence of the calm fullness makes her feel present as herself. The more the fullness, strength and calmness expand, the more she feels present, present as herself. She experiences herself as a being, a presence, a fullness. She is not an action or a reaction. She is not a feeling or a thought or an image, but a firm, strong, full, and exquisitely alive presence.

Intimacy

Late afternoon, just back from my office, after a full day of eventful teaching sessions with students. I lie down in bed, mildly tired. I can feel the psychic layers that I have taken on from students peeling off, one by one. As each layer peels away, it reveals its content—emotions, thoughts, images, physical tensions. This process leaves me clearer and lighter. The lightness opens further, revealing spaciousness. Consciousness manifests as empty, transparent space, light and clean.

In this spaciousness my own thoughts and feelings appear: a constellation of thoughts and subtle feelings, all related to images and impressions about my identity, about who I am. This psychic cluster, like a cloud in the spaciousness of mind, provides the mind with the familiar feeling of identity, an identity totally dependent on memories of my past experience. Contemplating the totality of the cluster, without taking an inner position about it, I recognize that it is a mental phenomenon. On seeing this, I become distinctly aware that it is external to me. The feeling-recognition is: "this is not me."

The focus of attention spontaneously shifts. The psychic cluster gently fades away, almost imperceptibly, like a cloud slowly dissipating. When it is gone, what is left is simplicity, a clear and simple sense of presence without self-reflection. There are no thoughts about the experience, no feelings about it, only the simplicity of presence. Clarity, space, stillness and lucidity bring a sense of a crisp cloudless sky around a snow-capped mountain top.

The sun is about to set, and the windows open on the East, so the bedroom is somewhat dark. The sun illuminates some of the hillside, while the rest is steadily cooled by the expanding gentle shade. The flowers in the pots outside the room appear bright; the green leaves glisten. Lucidity pervades everything: the flower pots, the trees, the distant clouds, the deep blue sky. All is pristine, undisturbed by wind or thought.

In the lucidity of space, a question appears, carefree and delighted: "And what is me?" Nothing recognizable by memory. I experience myself, without a feeling of self, as the simplicity of presence, which is now a simplicity of perception, a bare witnessing. There is no inner dialogue, and no commentary on what is perceived. The perceiving is without a perceiver, awareness without an observer. Without self-reflection, the simplicity of presence is merely the simplicity of witnessing. I am a witness of all in the field of vision, a witness with no inside. The witness is merely the witnessing. The only thing left from familiar experience is the location of witnessing, which seems to be determined by the location of the body. The body is relaxed and clear. The sense of the body is more of luminosity than of sensation, witnessed as part of the environment.

Time does not seem to pass; it has come to a stop. When the psychic constellation that has given me the familiar sense of identifying myself ceases, the sense of the passage of time is gone. In the simplicity of presence, time does not pass, for the sense of the passage of time is simply the continuity of the feeling of the familiar identity.

Simplicity of presence, when it is complete, is timelessness. Timelessness is completely being the simplicity of presence. Timelessness is not an idea, a thought in the mind. It is the fullness of the experience of presence of Being, pure and prior to thought or self-reflection.

A few days later . . .

Upon waking up in the morning, I find my attention riveted by a feeling of hurt in the heart. The hurt is warm and sad. It feels like the heart is wounded in its very flesh. The hurt leads to a gnawing sensation in the mobius, the subtle center at the sternum. The gnawing is painful; it feels physically grating, but also emotionally difficult. A frustrated feeling has become stuck at the lower part of the chest, turning into a gnawing sensation. I feel all this mixed with the feeling of hurt and sadness.

I contemplate the hurt, the sadness and the physical contraction. Holding all in awareness, while intimately feeling all of the nuances of the ongoing experience. The contemplating awareness embraces the content of experience with a feeling of warm kindness and with an attitude of curiosity, not knowing what the hurt is about, but interested to find out. The gnawing sensation responds to the motiveless inquiry, and begins to soften as the contraction at the mobius center relaxes, revealing an unexpected element to the sadness: loneliness. The hurt turns out to be the pain of feeling lonely. The feeling of loneliness wets the sadness with more tears, and the hurt expands into an emptiness underlying the sadness. Now it is deep, sad loneliness.

But why, why am I feeling lonely?

There does not seem to be any reason for it. I am still in bed, my wife, Marie, lying asleep beside me. I feel my affection for her, but this does not touch the sad loneliness. The loneliness continues even though I am not alone.

I get up, go to the bathroom to wash, the loneliness following me, filling the space of the bathroom with its teary sadness. The question continues to live, while I shave: what is making me feel lonely? Here, memory reminds me of the experience of the last few days, that of the simplicity of presence and witnessing. Reflecting on it, I intuit that there is a connection between the experience of simple presence and the feeling of loneliness. My curiosity intensifies, a throbbing sensation at the forehead begins to luminate.

The throbbing lumination at the forehead reveals itself to be a diamond-clear and colorful presence. The more passionate the naturally curious contemplation is about the loneliness, the more alive and brilliant becomes this presence, manifesting spacious and discerning clarity. I recognize the variegated, scintillating presence as the discriminating intelligence, the true nous [the dimension of universal concepts and the source of knowing, the "Divine Mind" or Gnosis], which appears as a presencing of the intensification of consciousness, at the center of the forehead, to reveal the meaning of experience. The intensification of inquiry coincides with a greater and more definite presence of the discriminating intelligence, revealing its exquisite sense of delicate precision.

The experience now is a field of sadness, loneliness and emptiness, combined with the memory of the simplicity of presence, all opening up to the scintillatingly alive presence of the nous. Insights begin to radiate out from the scintillating consciousness. Perceptually, the operation of the nous appears as a multicolored glittering radiance; affectively, it is a delicate and pleasant expansive clarity; cognitively, it is the spontaneous arising of insight.

The understanding unfolds: the sense of simplicity in the experience of presence is finding myself as the presence of Being, totally and purely, without thoughts or feelings about it. There is simplicity because there remains only the purity of presence, with no memory and no mind. This absence of mind, in the completeness of being presence, is tantamount to the absence of everything that mind carries. During the experience of the last few days I saw how the mind creates and carries the sense of familiar identity of the self, which it accomplishes through memory and self-reflection. What I did not see then, but was implicit in the experience, is that the mind carries also the sense of the other—of another person—again by using memory.

Here, I remember the insight of the object relation psychologists: the sense of self develops in conjunction with the sense of other, first the mother, then all others. The understanding is that the familiar sense of identity develops from early on within a field of object relations, always in relation to another person.

This sense of self becomes a felt continuity by the memories of these experiences of oneself coalescing into a fixed structure in the psyche. Hence, this psychic structure also contains the memories of interactions with significant others.

When I felt the sense of familiar identity disappear I did not see that this also meant the disappearance of all impressions of others. In other words, as the activity of the mind comes to a stop, all the feelings dependent on the internalized memories disappear. This understanding shows me that the sense of familiar identity always includes, explicitly or implicitly, the feeling of others. The feeling of self swims in an atmosphere of internalized relationships.

This normally ever-present atmosphere of an interpersonal world ceases in the experience of the simplicity of presence, allowing presence to be alone. This aloneness of presence is its simplicity. Recently I have been experiencing it as simplicity, but this experience shows me that I have unconsciously reacted to it as total aloneness.

Here, the feeling of emptiness deepens into a dark abyss, and the loneliness disappears into a singular state of aloneness, existential and fundamental. A hint of sadness remains, in the form of a subtle, warm feeling pervading the deepening emptiness. The throbbing presence at the forehead again scintillates brightly; this time emerald green outshines its other living colors. The sadness reveals associations with the state of aloneness: times in childhood when I was left alone. In the emptiness of the mind float memories of a sad and lonely child, left alone, sometimes forgotten.

Recognizing that the source of the feeling of loneliness is my association of the painful loneliness of the past with the state of aloneness of presence in the present, liberates the sadness, allowing it to evaporate, leaving a sense of transparent depth to the dark abyss, a spacious depth. The feeling is centered in the chest, as if the chest region has become void of everything, except for a subtle lightness which curiously feels deep. Feeling within the chest, inquiring with no goal in mind, I find no sense of solidity. The chest feels empty, but curiously quiet, peaceful and still. I recognize the state as a luminous black spaciousness, which is the unity of stillness and space. There is immaculate, glistening emptiness, but the emptiness has a sense of depth. The depth seems to be the felt aspect of the blackness of space. It is like looking into, and feeling into, starless deep space.

The depth, although void, has a soft texture, an exquisite gentleness. There is a sense of comfort, safety, and a carefree trust, as if the vastness of intergalactic space has mysteriously evolved into a gentle and loving medium. It is not a cold space, not an impersonal space, but a space that feels exactly like what the human soul has perennially longed for: the warmth of mother's breasts, the softness of delicate velvet, a quiet shining blissfulness, and an endless generosity.

My chest has become an opening into an infinitely deep and dark space, which feels clear and void of all extraneous things. Also, inseparable from the transparent voidness, is the presence of love itself. Now I can taste the pleasurable sweetness of love on my tongue, and throughout the whole chest cavity.

As I proceed to the dining room, I feel myself inseparable from the total stillness of this loving space. The mind is quiet and peaceful, the body relaxed and its movements easy. As I begin breakfast with Marie, the sweet quietness envelops us. We talk about the practical things of the day, but now I begin to recognize another dimension to the loving void.

At the beginning this seems to be related to our easy and simple conversation, where the peaceful sweetness divulges itself as a delicate contact between us, a subtle intimacy. I like the gentle intimacy, and awareness gently focuses on its exquisite sensation. There are lightness and depth, spaciousness and softness, clarity and sweetness. The feeling of intimacy is not new in my experience. However, I slowly realize that I feel intimate not only with Marie, but also with the food, with the tablecloth, with the chairs, even with the walls. I feel intimate with everything I am aware of, in an atmosphere of gentle quiet and relaxed openness. Everything seems to have now this quality of softness and contactfulness. More accurately, everything seems to be bathed in this intimate spaciousness, as if everything is sharing itself, with total generosity and complete openness.

Intimacy discloses itself as an inherent quality of this black inner space. The intimacy is not only a matter of me being intimate with another person, or with the environment. It is not a matter of a subject intimately relating to an object. The chest cavity is pervaded by the essence of intimacy, a black spaciousness inseparable from delicate lovingness.

At this point the jewel-like nous at the forehead manifests mostly black radiance, coextensive with the sensation of delicately faceted, satin, liquid energy.

The more I recognize that intimacy is a quality of spacious consciousness, the more distinctly I know it: velvet-fine openness, deep spaciousness, delicate softness, sweet stillness. The chest has become an entrance into an exquisitely heartful night sky. All of this distills itself into something unique and utterly human: intimacy. It is as if the space is a refined consciousness intimately in contact with its very nature at each point of its spaciousness. And this total openness and contact becomes an intimacy with everything, totally independent of mind and memory.

No loneliness and no sense of aloneness. Simplicity of Being has ushered me, through the door of aloneness, into its inherent intimacy.

◆

CHAPTER 3

THE SOUL

O NE OF THE BROADEST and most useful perceptions in the Diamond Approach is its understanding of the soul. Ali uses the term in the older sense in which it was used in spiritual and mystical traditions as the totality of consciousness or the self. The soul of the human being is the underlying consciousness of the individual, its living, intelligent awareness. It is the totality of the human being. All expressions of our aliveness, functioning, and consciousness are expressions of the soul.

It is the soul that digests experience and that is transformed in the human being through experiences. The soul is the site and container of individual experience. It is the fabric of experience. The soul is the means through which Being experiences itself. All content of awareness is content of the soul. Sensations, perceptions, emotions, thoughts, and concepts are all forms flowing within the soul. We could more accurately say that these experiences are the soul—the soul as a sensation, as an emotion, or as a concept. It is not outside these experiences, but their medium or substance. For instance, in the emotion of joy, it is the soul that takes on the qualities of happiness, elation, expansion, and lightness that we call joy. Joy is one of the potential qualities of the soul.

The soul can be compared to water that is shaped into an infinite variety of forms. In fact, water may be an especially good metaphor for the soul since its ancient root meaning is "coming from or belonging to the sea." Water takes the shape of the container into which it flows: a creek when it is between two narrow banks, a river when it is between two widely separated shores, or an ocean when it seems to go on forever. However, regardless of its shape, water is still the basic substance or medium of creeks, rivers, and oceans. To further the comparison to the soul, this water can be aware of itself as a creek, a river, or an ocean. Of course, water can also be dammed up, clouded by pollutants, asleep to itself. It is like the difference between seeing the water itself and seeing only its shape as a stream or waves. Or it is like viewing a painting and, rather than focusing on the shapes and color of the painting, seeing the texture and vibrancy of the canvas itself.

The term *soul* is used widely these days in personal and spiritual growth, notably in the useful work of James Hillman and Thomas Moore. Some people use it to refer to authenticity, aliveness, and immediacy, as when we say that certain art, food, or people have soul. Others contrast soul with spirit and use soul to refer to those experiences that are deeply meaningful and in touch with the life of the body and the world. They use *spirit* to refer more to transcendent and impersonal experiences and *soul* to refer more to immanent and personal experiences. The Diamond Approach uses this term in a more inclusive way to include the full range and depth of the human being. Soul does not refer to an enduring transcendent entity that is beyond our experience. Instead, it refers to our very consciousness itself.

CHARACTERISTICS OF THE SOUL

The soul is tremendously mutable and impressionable. Thus, it can feel immediate and alive, or transcendent and beyond life or death. As the fabric of experience, it takes on any texture, color, and pattern given it. At the same time, the soul can be experienced directly. Terms like *flow, aliveness, spontaneity, receptivity, potentiality, malleability, impressionability,* and *unfoldment* can be used to describe the intrinsic qualities of the soul. The soul feels like a flowing substance, like protoplasm that is alive and conscious. Given this malleability, the soul is affected in an exquisitely sensitive way by experience. Because of this, it can feel stuck, dead, and occluded, as well as fresh, alive, and refined.

Another way to say this is that the soul can be structured by personality or by Being. These structures shape the container of experience, determining its texture and flow. When the soul is structured by personality, it is structured in a defensive and fixated way. Thus, the personality's experience feels stiff, stuck, dead, reactive, afraid, and frustrating. This restricts the flow of experience, and life seems to be shallow, meaningless, and limited. Experience filtered through a rigid and defensive structuring of the soul is inauthentic; we are alienated from our world and from our lives.

Personality structures can be more or less rigid, of course. A personality that is less constricted is more open to experience, including experiences of its deeper nature. Still, any structure, even the healthiest, becomes a limitation if you hold on to it. One of the functions of the Diamond Approach is to soften, develop, and then integrate personality structures into the soul.

On the other hand, Being can also provide the patterns for the soul. Ali calls these patterns Essence, and when the soul is patterned by Essence, the flow of Being is free and unrestricted. The soul is then in its natural state: present, open, intelligent, and flowing.

When consciousness is open to Being, it is authentic. A soul that is more open will experience pleasure, love, and lightness more fully. It will experience grief, loss, and pain more fully as well. When the soul is more open and refined, there is less struggle or need to control the flow of reality. This means that difficult experiences will become less problematic. A soul that is more fluid and receptive experiences more fully whatever is present. There is a bittersweet poignancy in the passing of each moment as well as gratitude and fulfillment.

Yet an authentic life is also informed by the beauty and magnificence of the world. The life of the human being comes to be seen in its magnificence, richness, and mystery. Opening ourselves to the outflow of Being is really Being opening to itself. Even the simplest things are spiritual. Hanging out with friends, touching a leaf, making love, gazing at the far horizon—the ordinary reveals the extraordinary. We are at home in our lives.

Work on the Soul

The soul digests experience and is itself affected, changed, and transformed by experience. It is the consciousness that learns, grows, matures, and expands through our encounters with the world. The soul can also be blocked and constricted. Since it needs to be awakened, healed, developed, clarified, refined, and transmuted in psychological and spiritual work, the soul is an important and far-reaching focus of spiritual work.

Many kinds of work on the soul allow it to be more open, more refined, and more transparent, allowing for experience that is fuller, richer, more alive, more genuine, and more authentic. Living more fully in our bodies, becoming more available and honest in our relationships, healing unresolved traumas, removing the barriers to fulfillment in our work lives, engaging our life transitions with confidence and openness, as well as meditation, contemplation, and Inquiry are important aspects of awakening the soul to its possibilities.

We need to free the soul so it can respond more fully to transforming experiences. Releasing, healing, and freeing the soul releases its spontaneity, aliveness, and sensitivity. This is important in its own right, and it is critical to doing the work of self-realization and spiritual development. As the soul is more clear and open, it is more spacious, more sensitive, and less thick. Experiences can have more impact. This can help us understand those times when we have had wonderful peak experiences that did not leave much of a permanent, trans-formative effect. Because our souls are usually structured by personality, these experiences are lost in the inertia of our usual ways of thinking and feeling. As our souls become more open, inertia is replaced by the soul's intrinsic permeability.

Any work that helps free the soul will undercut this inertia and allow these kinds of experiences to be taken in. It can then have a more lasting effect. Furthermore, when the soul is not open and receptive to experience, spiritual work can seem dull, heavy, and only serious. Spiritual work can be difficult, but it can also be done with enthusiasm.

Psychological healing, the recovery of aspects of the soul abandoned in childhood (or the "soul child," as Ali calls it), the realization of Essence, and the work on the Boundless or nondual dimensions of Being are linked through the soul. The soul is the container for experience in all of these realms. Re-gardless of what level or depth we are working on, it is still the soul that is being affected. Meditation, deep psychotherapy, bodywork, work on the "inner child," soul recovery, and espe-cially Inquiry (as in the Diamond Approach) are all useful in the work of opening the soul. Rather than disconnected prac-tices or sequential steps, they are all seen by the Diamond Ap-proach as aspects of one process revealing the deeper nature of the soul, purifying it, and supporting its unfoldment.

The Soul and Resistance

Although it is the basic nature of the soul to be affected by experience, it also has the capacity to develop resistances to its effects. When the soul is structured primarily by primitive structures, its primary orientation becomes avoiding pain and seeking pleasure. When this is the case, we are less open to our experience and more concerned with getting our personality needs met. We find resistance and inertia in the soul rather than openness and aliveness.

Resistances usually have very specific textures and effects. The cruel, and often clever, judgments of the inner critic or superego are a kind of resistance that shows up early (as well as later) in spiritual work. These inner attacks may feel as if you were being bludgeoned with a club or wounded in your heart with a razor-sharp knife, but they generally bring a sense of a wound or cut. Closing yourself off to this wound closes your soul to its life and expansion.

Other kinds of resistance may feel like rubber. Experiences, confrontations, or insights are "bounced back" instead of being taken in. The structures of the soul say, "I will take this in only so far, and then I will push it away." The harder you try to get through that resistance in a head-on way, the more the rubber pushes back. Another kind of resistance seems like iron, especially in the head. Using our familiar mental patterns to resist, we may feel as if our heads were made of iron—heavy, thick, and impenetrable. A state that feels like lead is also a common form of resistance. Here we find a type of lethargy and indolence that weighs down any kind of movement, flow, or expansion.

Work on the soul is necessary to remove these resistances. To the extent that your personality structures are projected onto your spiritual work, the soul can directly inhibit your growth and realization. When you encounter difficulties in your spiritual work, you are likely to project your parental voices onto that work. Invitations to spiritual realization may seem like criticisms when the superego comes in. The spiritual journey may seem to you to be cruelly punishing or impossibly distant, and your resistances will arise. Such issues, projections, and resistances will come up throughout the spiritual search.

Understanding the blocks of the soul and releasing it from these resistances, veils, and barriers are important in allowing spiritual work to be direct and effective. In their work with individual students, Diamond Approach teachers most often work first with the resistance itself and then with the content of the experience that was being resisted. A good deal of the initial work with Diamond Approach groups is also devoted to resistance. Using the perspective of Inquiry, the basic aim is seeing the action of the resistance, how it manifests, what it is trying to avoid, and its long-term constrictive consequences. As with other aspects of the Diamond Approach, the work on the soul's resistances is done with an integration of compassion, perseverance, and guidance.

The Diamond Approach works to refine and develop the soul. As the soul matures and develops, it gains new qualities and characteristics, developing and unfolding into deeper levels and dimensions. It is more open to expressing a greater range and depth of Essential states. When Ali teaches about unfoldment, consciousness, awakening, and realization, he is teaching about the soul. The practices and methods of the Diamond Approach are ways of working to clarify, liberate, and purify the soul.

In the first selection, Ali gives a flavor of the soul in its original, primitive, and unrefined state. He goes on to discuss the development and maturation of the soul as an important part of the work of the Diamond Approach. This selection is from a talk given to students who have been studying the Diamond Approach for about a year. In the second selection, he clarifies how he is using the terms *self* and *soul* in his writing on self-realization. He points to some of the characteristics of the soul, including its dynamism, flow, and intrinsic consciousness. Here, *self-realization* means the soul's realization of its intrinsic nature and possibilities. Since these passages are drawn from Ali's book on true identity (*The Point of Existence;*

see Chapter 8), they focus on narcissism. His forthcoming book on the soul will expand this discussion to include other Essential aspects and dimensions.

The Swamp Thing

Tonight I'll talk about the Swamp Thing. Have you seen the movie about the Swamp Thing, the monster that turns out to be a good guy? I was trying to find the title of our talk and thought this fits. I'm going to speak about the story of the soul: what it is, its relationship to the soul child, and how this segment of our work is a matter of learning to civilize the Swamp Thing.

We can look at our work as accelerating and supporting the evolutionary process of the development of the human being. To really consider the soul means you're working with the development of the human being because the concept of the soul gives us a way of understanding the work of the Diamond Approach as a maturation, a development, and an evolution of our humanness. We start, in some sense, as Swamp Things. In some very deep subterranean place in us, we're very much like Swamp Things. Basically, you can say a large part of the work on the soul has to do with coming to terms with that primitive part of us, the primitive, animal, instinctive life force.

We notice that at the beginning of life the child has an Essential nature that is a sense of purity, lovingness, and innocence. There's a capacity for pleasure, a contentment. We also notice what happens when you cross a little kid. That innocence turns into animal-like rage. When the child is not given what it wants, the greed and the want becomes passionate. It's not, "Will you please give me this? Thank you." The child doesn't do that. It just grabs for what it wants. When it's had enough it just leaves. It is the way an animal is. We could say, "What innocence!" It's true it is innocence, but we notice there is an animal quality to the child, especially a very young child.

At the beginning of our life, we see the soul. We're seeing the aliveness, the consciousness, the beingness that we're calling the soul. It has its purity and Essential nature, but it also has a very instinctive, primitive, quite responsive, and quite alive nature. That instinctive, primitive, alive nature has impediments. The softness, the gentleness, and the innocence could turn easily into anger, rage, greed, or intense fear. It can quickly become intense desire, protest, vengeance, and all the intense passions that human beings have.

The soul is our experience of ourselves, what we are, including the totality of everything about us. This is true for us not only as babies, but even now as adults, too. We're always the soul. The soul is the experiencing of consciousness, or the psychic organism. It is the experiencer and the site of experience. It not only experiences and feels itself, but it is also responsive and alive. When you experience the soul, when you finally discriminate what the soul is, you recognize that it's you and that you're always the soul. You cannot be anything but the soul. The soul is you that is living, experiencing, thinking, feeling, responding. It is a psychic organism in the sense that it is an organism of experience, awareness, contact, feeling, responsiveness, desire, and action. It is a unified, total wholeness that is alive and energetic, that feels and acts as a unit.

As very young children, that quality of aliveness and the primordial presence of a consciousness is clear. However, after we go through the usual civilizing process, that quality of the soul is lost because of the civilizing process. We still continue feeling the soul, but we end up feeling it as rarefied and diminished. We lose the sense of being unified and whole so much that we merely experience thoughts, feeling, actions, and desires as if they are happening by themselves. We're not feeling the organism that is the site and source of all of these. But we are still that organism. That experience has been conditioned to such a degree that this organism has almost become not there, in some sense. We're just aware of some kind of insubstantial awareness. We don't recognize that this awareness is really part and parcel of a living, responsive presence. When you experience the free soul, you feel as if your whole organism is one living muscle that acts as a unit and feels as a unit and desires as a unit and loves as a unit. When it loves, it wants. When it wants, it enjoys wanting. When it gets what it wants, it can feel satisfied in a very deep, very physical way—the way an animal is satisfied.

At the beginning our soul is not very different from the soul of an animal. That's why it is said in some traditions that the beginning of the human development is the animal soul. The animal soul means our original condition before it developed and progressed to a more refined and spiritual sense. The soul is a spiritual organ and a spiritual presence, but remember what spiritual means. Spiritual doesn't mean "airy fairy." Spiritual means what's real, what is.

At the beginning, our spirituality has an animal quality. It has the purity of Essence. Essence is part of the potential of our soul when we are relaxed, contented, satisfied. There's a contentment, a fullness, a purity, and an innocence. But when hunger strikes the animal comes out. There was a time in all of us when we were hungry, really hungry. I mean your stomach contracts and all your organism is hungry, all through. When you see the breast, it is this wonderful, beautiful, wish-fulfilling food. All of you becomes like one big stomach. It's not just the mouth that has an orgasm. The whole organism can have an orgasm.

We need to recognize or reconnect with our soul because our Essential nature is really the Essence of that soul. The Essence, the purest spiritual qualities, are the potential of this soul. The soul goes through its maturation, evolution, and development. It starts as an animal soul, goes on through what's called a human soul, and becomes a spiritual soul. That's a natural process of maturation. The soul begins as the animal soul, which means an organ, not of consciousness, but of desire. An organ of responsiveness, an organ of action, a primitive life form. This could be experienced many ways. You can experience yourself as just an organic kind of living presence, or you can experience yourself more like fluid and moving and free, the way a jellyfish is. Or you could experience yourself more primitive than that, almost like an amoeba. A big one. But when we're experiencing ourselves as jellyfish or as amoebae, formless but alive, responsive but without structure, we're experiencing our soul in its primitive form before development. It starts at the beginning as very simple, very almost like plasmatic, primal substance. Primal ooze. That's why I call it the Swamp Thing. It is primitive in the sense a jellyfish is primitive compared to a lion. It's not formed, not developed, not structured. With that come all the animal instincts, for instance for food, for safety. There is an instinct for pleasure and an instinct for movement with also a potential for growth and development, for evolution.

When we see the baby, in some sense there's no structure. The child is sometimes all innocence and at other times like a monster, yelling and screaming. All these possibilities are there. It's a very fluid thing that is moving with the situation. It's very changeable, very dynamic, very responsive. This soul grows and develops as the body also grows and develops. Little by little that organism becomes more like a person with definite characteristics and structures.

We start not only as the living substance that is also consciousness, but we have the life force and we have our aggression and we have our power. We have the innate, organic intelligence that children have. It is a very brilliant kind of intelligence, the way an animal is intelligent. We are responsive and sensitive to our environment and to other people. There's a spontaneity without a premeditation about what we're going to feel, what we're going to do, what we're going to want. It's a very organismic and responsive kind of dynamism.

When children start crawling and walking, they need control in some sense. Not in the sense of being bad but in the sense that somebody needs to direct and help manage these impulses. You can't leave that child in your living room without attending to it. If you do for twenty minutes, God knows what will happen to your furniture, to your TV, to your desk. It will be like leaving a monkey in the house, basically. That shows you the primitive animal quality which is there at the beginning. Of course it is cute and wonderful and all that, but it stops being cute when it messes up your desk. That's when the civilizing process happens. That organism at the beginning only knows desires. The animal soul is run by its desires; when those are gone, it is contented, Essence arises, and the little baby is an angel. One moment it's a devil, and the next it's an angel.

There's nothing wrong with this primitiveness. That's how human beings are at the beginning. It is that primitive soul that needs to develop, evolve, and mature to go to the spiritual stage of being a complete human being. That's really the evolutionary process. Getting rid of your personality will not make everything fine. The moment you get rid of your personality your soul will come out. "Now I can do my thing," it says.

In working with the soul we want to get in touch with that organism, with our aliveness in its original form. At the beginning of the civilizing process, the heart of the soul, the living, responsive, genuine, real part, is suppressed. Children do need to learn, to develop, to grow up. They can't just go around doing whatever they feel like doing. There needs to be some kind of regulation and discipline so this organism will learn what is good for it and what is not, what really hurts other people, what people can tolerate, how to get along with others.

The child needs to learn all these things, and most parents, since they never developed themselves, never had the chance to go through their own true mature development in a healthy, balanced, natural way. They have to do it to the child the way it was done to them and that happens by becoming the authority. Most of the time it's done in a moralistic, judgmental, critical, rejecting, hostile way. It's not done with love and understanding. Most parents don't have their true firmness and will. They become harsh, hard and punishing to control the child. Or, without a genuine will, a parent may not say no at all, giving a child no support and letting the child be in charge. Many parents vacillate between being too harsh and too permissive.

Young children try to get rid of what the parents say they shouldn't do, and so they repress the wants, the impulses, the aliveness, and the exuberance to become what they believe their parents wanted them to be. What is repressed is really the living core of the soul. That part disappears, and we start defining ourselves through the eyes of the environment instead of being these spontaneous, creative impulses coming from within. That pure but animal-like, vital, instinctive, passionate, zesty nature is what we call the soul child. It is how you experienced yourself before you were civilized, before you learned what to be to fit into the civilized order. The soul child is the last time we experienced ourselves as our living soul. That living core got suppressed, and after awhile we forgot even the feeling of what's it like to be a living, conscious soul.

We want to find the soul child. Remember, we're not trying to reconnect with the soul child just to have a child within us. What we want is to connect with our soul. The way we go about connecting with our soul is to go back to the last way we experienced it, and that happens to be the soul child. As we experience the soul child, we start recognizing the soul. Recognizing the soul will start its inner Essential qualities manifesting, and that will help it develop and mature to attain its capacities, its qualities, its faculties.

There is a lot more to the human soul than most people know. To become a mature human being, you need to find your own soul child, connect with your own soul, and learn how to deal with your soul so it will mature and develop in a refined, human, empathic, sensitive, kind, loving way without losing its aliveness and passion and zest. That's not an easy thing. A large part of our work has to do with that. Reconnecting with our Essential qualities is necessary to do that job. But the first thing we need to do is we need to deal with the repression.

The more we are able to experience the soul child without

letting it act out its impulses, the more that part of us becomes alive, becomes integrated, matures, and develops. The soul child is not something that will continue being a child forever. Your soul is a part of you that hasn't developed because it got arrested because of the repression or the splitting off. You want to reconnect with that part, and as you reconnect and it becomes the core of your inner life, it will start maturing, unfolding and developing. After awhile it's not really a child, but it continues having the child-like qualities of passion, playfulness, and delight. It will also have refinement and subtlety and peacefulness and discrimination and compassion. That's what we mean by the words *complete human being:* an expanded awareness, an efficiency in action, an intelligence.

What happens is more complex than this actually. The way I am saying it is still simple, and I'm not taking into account all the elements. The more the Essential qualities arise, the more you have a strength and a patience and a courage so that even when you're trembling, shaking in your boots, you're still able to be present and to observe. Having the strength and the capacity does not mean not getting too scared. It means you are courageous long enough to allow the fear to be strong. Fear is just an example. Sometimes you have intense rage or lot of hurt or deep sadness. It could be very deep. When the soul is really active, when you feel sad, you don't just feel a little sadness, a little trembling, a few tears. You feel as if you are an ocean of tears, a deep, profound ocean of tears, but it doesn't overwhelm you because you have enough experience and enough wisdom to know that it is fine.

As it is freed, the soul has more movement, flow, dynamism and an energy to it. And Essence, remember, is the inner nature of the soul, not something apart from it. Qualities within the soul that are developed in response to the environment sometimes can dominate the soul. Essence is the soul experiencing itself in an Essential way. Knowing this, we must still start with what we have and that is mostly an animal or child soul. Working with our desires, impulses, and reactions is the way to begin so that the soul can eventually know its Essential nature.

Self and Soul

In order to pursue our exploration of self-realization, we must elucidate how we are using the word *self*. Our use of the word is unusual in that it refers to an actual ontological presence, not a construct. This emphasis on the actual presence of what is here as the self, rather than on the content of the constructed aspects of the field of awareness, is a crucial aspect of our method of exploration and of our theoretical view.

In our view, the self is a living organism that constitutes a field of perception and action. This is what we call "soul." Fundamentally, it is an organism of consciousness, a field of awareness capable of what we call experience—experience of the world and of self-reflective awareness of itself. In *The Point of Existence* we will use the words *soul* and *self* somewhat interchangeably; the meaning of either word is always that defined above. Our understanding of soul is not that it is a split off or special part of the self that is more esoteric or ethereal or spiritual than any other elements. We use the word *soul* to describe the entire organism. This usage reflects the fact that the deepest perception of the self reveals that the entire Being of the self is of the same nature as that which, in conventional reality, is relegated to the spiritual or the divine. As our discussion progresses we will sometimes use *self* and *soul* in slightly different ways. We will predominantly use the word *self,* however, because its connotation can include many aspects of the total self, including its structures. We will use the word *soul* more to connote the dynamic, alive presence of the self as distinguished from the structures of the self which pattern this presence. It is important to allow a slight ambiguity in our use of these words in order for our understanding to be faithful to the deeper perspective. The soul, as an alive conscious presence, is ultimately not separate from the structures which form the ego. It is when they are taken as the self's identity that these structures alienate the soul's experience from awareness of its true nature.

The most striking aspects of this organism which is the self, or soul, are its malleability, sensitivity, intelligence, and dynamism. The soul can take many forms; it is not a rigid structure but a flowing, conscious presence with certain inherent capacities and faculties. The soul learns and the soul acts. The soul is an actual and real ontological presence; it is not simply a product of the body, as much modern thought would define it. However, it is not necessary for the purposes of this book to completely clarify the relationship of the self to the body. Even if the soul were somehow a product of the body, these qualities of consciousness and dynamism of the soul would remain demonstrable, even obvious.

What is conventionally known as the psyche is part of this self (or soul). The mind is part of the self, manifesting the capacity to remember, to think, to imagine, to construct and integrate images, to discriminate, analyze, synthesize, and so on. The feelings are part of the self: the capacity to desire, to choose, to value, to love.

In addition to the realms of mental, emotional, and physical experience, the self has access to the realm of Being, that is, it can experience directly rather than indirectly its own presence as existence. The conventional realms are involved in and generally affected by the experience of Being, but when the dimension of Being is experienced there is a profound difference in one's perspective. The reason we have the capacity to experience Being is that the self is an actual ontological presence, a presencing of Being, not simply a construct, and this presence has the capacity to be self-aware. Thus, for the self to become directly aware of the realm of Being is for it to directly experience its own nature.

◆

CHAPTER 4

SPACE

W HETHER OUR PATHS take us into psychotherapy, spiritual work, or self-guided experiments with consciousness exploration, two states soon arise. First, we generally find a sense of emptiness, deficiency, disorientation, or weakness. We discover that much of our everyday experience is discolored by a feeling of constriction or a subtle kind of imprisonment. Our lives seem founded in limitations; everywhere we turn are boundaries.

We also eventually find a sense of spaciousness. It may be the result of an emotional release or the consequence of a deep insight. It might occur suddenly with a discharge of tension, or it might slowly creep into the periphery of our awareness. This spacious state brings an openness, an expansion, and a relief from constrictions. It is accompanied by a lightness, a greater sense of internal freedom, a reduction of mental anguish, and a sense of much greater potential and possibility than we had known before.

We may come to discover pretty early in our search that giving space to our experience helps. Whether it is physical pain, emotional distress, anger in a relationship, or confusion, when we let there be space in our experience, it moves. We discover as well that when we try to reject or avoid our suffering, it only gets more entrenched. We see that space is on our side.

The understanding of these two states and their connection is an important foundation for the work of the Diamond Approach. The work on space and self-image is fundamental for lasting transformation and change, and it shows up throughout the Diamond Approach. For this reason, Ali devoted one of his first books, *The Void: A Psychodynamic Investigation of the Relationship between Mind and Space,* entirely to the subject of space, and it was the focus of his first training retreat for Diamond Approach teachers.

THE SELF-IMAGE

Self-image is used in the Diamond Approach (as it is used in much of the literature of psychoanalytic psychology) to refer to the conceptual framework that is used to define the self. It is much more than merely the social mask we present to others. It also includes our inner view of ourselves and our body image. The self-image is not innate but develops through our interactions with the world, significant others, and our bodies. We come to be attached to our self-image, and we take it to be who (and all) we really are.

We all use a wide variety of mental structures, memories, plans, and images to conduct our lives successfully. To be most useful, our mental representations need to be in touch with reality. When we approach any situation with a fixed structure based on past experiences, we are bound to be somewhat out of touch with the reality of the present situation. Our perceptions, behaviors, and relationships will be less responsive, less appropriate, and less effective. By the same token, they will also be more reactive, more forced, and more frustrating.

The basic nature of the mind is space, unstructured and open. This means, too, that our underlying experience of ourselves will be spacious and open to whatever arises in this space. When we identify with mental structures and their underlying boundaries, however, this space becomes bounded and restricted. The self-image is the collection and integration of those structures and boundaries that are developed in the process of ego development. The self-image, then, is the sum total of those mental structures that we use to define ourselves.

These boundaries divide inner space and the flow of experience that arises in it into discrete objects and actions. Special problems arise when we then use these mental structures to define ourselves. We are restricted in how we can respond best and how much we can develop. We become predisposed to certain patterns, and other possibilities continue to elude us.

This discussion of space and self-image mirrors somewhat the understanding of the soul and its structuring. When we focus on soul, we see Being as the flow, aliveness, and spontaneity of an individual consciousness. We also see how that soul or consciousness is bounded, occluded, and rigidified by identifications with personality structures. In a similar way, when we focus on space, Being appears as openness and clarity. We see space as bounded and constricted by self-images. It is important to consider the soul and space on their own terms, yet these two concepts offer two different, complementary perspectives on Being.

SPACE AND INNER CHANGE

For the great majority of mature adults, our usual state is to be identified with our self-image. Until there is a change in self-image, there can only be a linear elaboration of what has gone before, including the struggle, frustration, confusion, and pain. Furthermore, there can be no change in the self-image without the dissolution of the boundaries that constitute the self-image. When we dissolve the boundaries that make up those self-images, we experience space. Space then allows the self-image to loosen and change.

Even though its end result may be in the service of growth, the disidentification that leads to space is unsettling and disturbing. For disidentification from self-images to be helpful, a person needs a strong and well-developed capacity to integrate new and unusual states. If the dissolution of boundaries is too radical compared to a person's capacity to hold these states, it will be traumatic, and it will reinforce the defensive boundaries and resistances. On the other hand, given the necessary support to move into these states, growth and unfoldment can happen. This is partly the function of a teacher who understands personality structure and the deeper levels of emptiness and space. Even more, this capacity to work with disidentification comes as part of personal maturity and integration.

EMPTINESS AND SPACE

Psychoanalytic psychologists have seen emptiness as a key indicator of unhealthy and unintegrated ego structures. In the typical psychological view, we should avoid emptiness by strengthening and integrating our boundaries and psychological structures. On the other hand, many spiritual systems, especially Buddhism, have seen emptiness as the objective nature of reality and the truth behind any sense of self or identity. By bringing together these two views, the Diamond Approach helps us understand this apparent contradiction and use the insights of both approaches.

The Diamond Approach recognizes two kinds of emptiness: space and deficient emptiness. The first is the open and clear nature of Being. The second is what Ali calls a hole.

Deficient emptiness comes from the loss of Essence in ego development. Ego development is both a cause and a consequence of the loss of Essence. As Essence is abandoned in the psychological development of the young child and as our contact with Essence is lost, we sense the lack of Being. This lack is felt as a hole in our psyches, as if some part of ourselves were missing. We feel empty in a deficient way. Ego structures and self-images develop (in part) to avoid the resulting sense of deficient emptiness. Yet they can never fill the emptiness because what is missing is not a self-image but Essence. Therefore, ego structures and self-images contain, at their core, deficient emptiness.

Because of this, any dissolving or melting of a self-image brings to consciousness the hole that was covered over by the self-image. This hole is really space seen through the filter of mental structures, mistaken beliefs, feelings, memories, and misunderstanding. Without these structures, deficient emptiness is revealed as space. Space does not feel deficient. Although it is empty, nothing is missing.

Holes arise not from the loss of personality structure but from our abandonment of Being. Loss of a self-image or any ego structure only exposes the deficient emptiness that was at the core of that self-image. This allows it to be understood and dissolved. The problem is not the loss of the personality structure, as most psychologists believe, but the fact that deficient emptiness is at the core of the personality. As unpleasant and frightening as this may be, on the other side of this deficient emptiness lies space, clarity, and freedom.

TYPES OF SPACE

In his teaching, Ali has described a dozen different types or grades of space, each with its own phenomenology and psychodynamics. Here, I will briefly describe four. All types of space have a sense of emptiness and spaciousness, and they are all connected to the dissolution of a boundary. The particular boundary or mental structure that is dissolved and the related self-image from which we disidentify give each type of space its particular characteristics.

The clear space is the one most easily and often experienced initially. It is the sense of expansion, lightness, and clarity that I have been referring to so far. The specific issue that blocks it relates to a felt deficiency in ability and capacity. It is the sense of castration or being cut off from your source of energy and vitality. In terms of body image, this feels like a hole in the genital area. This hole is not related to your actual body or to your gender. When the genital hole is experienced, you often feel a disintegration and a fear of falling apart. However, when this issue is explored deeply and the genital hole is accepted, the clear space comes. In terms of psychodynamic structures, the clear space is related to our mental images of ourselves and our concerns about how we appear to others and in the world. When this issue is seen through, clear space appears.

The black space is also felt as empty and light, but instead of being clear, it feels like blackness. It has a definite, though subtle, quality of peace, quiet, and silence about it. Its issue is the loss of identity and the fear that you will no longer be who you are.

The next type is clear dense space. To our ordinary experience, this seems like a riddle: how can empty space be dense? Yet it feels like an emptiness that is at the same time full, immense, and powerful. You are in touch with an unlimited spacious presence. This kind of space is related to the sense of physicality, and its issues arise in connection with a fear of the loss of the physical body and physical death.

The fourth type of space seems even more unlikely. It is an experience of black dense space. This space is connected to the fear of not existing at all. In the clear dense space, the boundaries of the body are gone, but there is still a subtle experience of identity. With black dense space, the issue is the fear of not existing at all, the fear of death. Therefore, when this issue is seen and understood and the identification with the internal sensations of the body are dissolved, black dense space arises. It is the experience of being a still, silent, immense mountain with the quality of space.

Other types of space are described, too, each with a set of psychological issues and each with its own qualities. All are related to different and more subtle aspects of identity. In other spiritual systems, some of these deeper types of space have been called *samadhi* or *sunyata*. Ali's book *The Void* describes these in detail.

WORKING WITH SPACE

There are several specific ways of working with space in the Diamond Approach. Since the experience of space is subtle, mindfulness and awareness practices are important. Awareness both requires and cultivates space. However, simply refining your awareness, in and of itself, is not enough for most of us to do the necessary work on space. Space will arise, but in time, it is filled again with self-images and other psychological structures.

We can also explore self-images by exploring our feelings and how we see ourselves and the world. Working with space means exploring one self-image after another. There are many layers of self-images and many layers, types, and grades of space. As a particular self-image dissolves, space arises, followed by the Essential aspect that was lost. This is replaced by another, more subtle self-image, which we then identify. This new identification can even be an identification with a mental representation of Essence. For example, experiencing the Essential quality of strength will bring a certain state. However, if we form an idea of this state and identify with the idea, we will have a new self-image. Exploring this deeper self-image, in turn, leads to a different, deeper layer of space.

In studying the phenomenon of space, we get a sense of the full sweep of the Diamond Approach. This brief overview has gone from familiar experiences of lightness and relief following an intellectual insight or an emotional release to an oxymoron like *black dense space*. However, these descriptions will be clear to those whose experience has led them into such states. The Diamond Approach offers understanding and methods that will allow serious students to test these statements in their own experience.

Two selections from Ali's writings are included here to illustrate this understanding of space and its role in psychological and spiritual work. The first is a general overview given to a group of Ali's students. In this passage, he focuses on the boundaries of space and our attachment to our self-images and identities. He also refers to deeper levels of space. In this selection, he is referring to all the types of space as *the void*. The second selection describes in detail some aspects of the direct experience of space. It includes several case studies as examples of different qualities of space and some of the issues related to it.

A note about terminology for readers not familiar with psychology: We are using several terms interchangeably—*psychoanalytic psychology, psychodynamic psychology,* and *depth psychology*—which in other contexts can be considered different theoretical perspectives. They all refer to the broad orientation in modern psychology that began with Freud and that has been significantly amplified and expanded by others. The Diamond Approach uses primarily the work of the ego psychologists, object relations theorists, and self psychologists. It focuses on the conscious and unconscious forces that affect us and especially the development of these forces in early childhood.

Attachment and Space

One of our deepest attachments is to our self-image, both how we see ourselves and how others see us. Our self-image is who we think we are, how we want to be, what we want to have in our life—whether it's a house that looks a certain way, a certain lover or mate who fills certain criteria. "I'm a good person and deserve this," or "I'm a bad person." The self-image we are attached to is often negative. Everyone has some negative self-image. If you're attached to being good, then you're always finding proof that you're a good person. You might be attached to a self-image of being good, strong, powerful, rich, beautiful, popular, being married, single, etc. This is the most superficial layer, and it's where most people live. The most common level of consciousness is focused on this superficial image level.

We usually identify with our self-image; we think that's who we are. This question of identity with what we think we are is at the root of attachment. What we ultimately want is to fight for who we really are, to actualize, protect, and defend who we really are. We want to make what we really are permanent and, depending on our knowledge of what we actually think we are, that's what we get attached to.

In the beginning, identity manifests as the self-image, and most of humanity seems to be concerned with this level. Your identity is very much invested in the image, how things look on the outside, and that's what you're attached to. The self-image gets fed by myriad attachments, from your car to your friends, from your interests, likes and dislikes to your ideas and feelings, your philosophies, all of your conscious awareness at any particular time. The work we do here, on the other hand, is on the dissolution of the self-image. What we mean here by dissolution is simply seeing that it isn't actually there. The dissolution of a certain identity is finally seeing that it is not really who you are, that the life that you have created around you is not really you. You believe that you can't exist without it; that without these ideas, these things, these attachments, you would not be you. "How would I know myself?" you wonder. "How would anyone know me?"

So the first level of attachment goes along with the first level of identity. It has to do with your ID cards. Just seeing that, "Oh, I believe that is me," and checking, "Is that really me?" will make the identity more transparent. The sincerity and the understanding dissolve the self-image, just as any untruth dissolves when the truth is seen. When any self-image changes there is a sense of freedom, the emergence of what we call space.

When there is space, there are no pictures, no boundaries. An image requires boundaries; it's a picture of who you are. So space erases your boundaries; it erases the picture on your driver's license, so to speak. You come to know yourself without the card. When you have no picture of yourself, there is space, the first level of the void.

At the next level of attachment, the core of the self-image is the body image. At the deepest level, your self-image is based on physical reality, the body image. When I say "body image," I include in that the shape of your body, how you feel about it, everything about your body, the organs of your body and the functions of your body. When you let go of the external card-holder identity, you find that then your identity is based on your body image, so you sense yourself, feel yourself, pay attention to yourself and feel that you know yourself more intimately. If you think you're beautiful, you like yourself; if you think you're not beautiful, you don't like yourself. You're fat or you're thin, you've got the right nose but the wrong mouth, or vice versa. These are the obvious body image concerns; it is part of the self-image, a kernel around which the rest of the self-image is built. It is attachment to physical things from the image perspective. The image of physical objects is present, not only image in the sense of shape, but also in terms of feeling, function, and relationship to your body.

If you go to the level of dealing with the physical or the body image, you will see that your body image is not accurate. Most people don't see their bodies, even in terms of shape, the way they really are. From these distortions in our self-image we build all kinds of psychological self-image compensations: I want to be beautiful, dress this way, cut my hair like this, have certain kinds of friends, have this kind of environment around me, get the best fashions, the whole thing. But at the bottom of it is a certain misperception of the body image. We need to understand the body image, to actually see what is really there, because the identity is very much involved with it. Understanding the body image, seeing your unconscious body image, contrasting it with what is actually there, corrects the misunderstanding. It will also eliminate the attachments, because the attachments arise from this misunderstanding. And this will bring in the next level of the void, what we call the dense space, because the body is dense compared to the self, and it is felt or sensed in this way. So another level of space will come that will erase or correct the body image by understanding the body image, which will itself eliminate the attachments to the body image, attachments on the level of the physical image. Now the truth emerges that I am not my physical image. First we free our identity, our external self-image, then we free ourselves from the external body image.

The next layer of identity is what we call the internal body image, or identification with the body regardless of the image, attachment to the body itself. Internal body image forms the core of the identity at this level, because of identification with the actual sensation of the body, the actual feelings in the body. It forms the core of both the body image and the self-image, and you're in touch with it most of your life. The inner sensations of the body—how it feels, the warmth or cold, harshness or softness, pleasure or pain, the flow and rigidity, the tension and relaxation—all become part of the identity.

This identity with the internal body image creates attachment to the body itself, to physical existence itself. You need to understand that this is not your identity. You are moving beyond an image here; these are your physical "innards." This identity is more intimate. You need to correct the common misunderstanding that to be your body, or to have your body, you have to hold on to it. You find out at some point when you're studying your attachment to your body, that you believe you have to hold on to your body to have it. You believe you need tensions in order to feel your body. If you were to completely relax, you would feel you were going to lose it, float away, so you grab on! That grabbing is the tension, and going deep inside that tension you will feel the actual stuff of attachment, which is hell.

So you need to come to an understanding of your relationship to your body, how you identify with your body and your attachment to your body as a result of that identification. You think your body is you, and you hold on to it for dear life, so you're never relaxed. This level includes all the attachments to all the bodily pleasures, and the negative attachments to all the physical pains. It includes sexual pleasure, physical contact pleasure, movement pleasure, stillness pleasure, all the realms of bodily attachment to pleasure and lack of it. Attachment to the body then is not just attachment to the physical body, but also to what the physical body means to you, all the pleasures and the comforts and the safety you believe it gives you. There is nothing wrong with these things; it's the attachment to them that creates the misunderstanding that is experienced as frustration and hell. I'm not saying you shouldn't want all these pleasures; that's not the point. The point is, the attachments to them will inevitably cause suffering.

Becoming free from this attachment has to do with becoming free from the attachment to pleasure, all kinds of pleasure. It is the loss of attachment to physicality, to your body from the inside. It's not a matter of image here, but of direct sensation, direct feeling. This identification is very intimate; it is something you've lived with all your life, and you always believe it's you. Ultimately, it gives you comfort. When you see this identification for what it is, it also will dissolve, because it isn't any more real than your driver's license identity.

This realization, in turn, brings in a new space, a new awareness of the void, what we call "death space." At this point a person experiences what is called death. It is what happens when somebody dies physically. They actually disconnect from the body. Death is a deep, dark, black emptiness. Of course, this death space can be experienced in life. You don't have to physically die; all that is required is to lose the physical attachment to the body, and the death space will be there. You will know what death is, you will know that you are not the body, and then the identification with the body will be lost. You will know what it's like not to be connected with the body. At a certain level of realization, if you are conscious when you're physically dying, then you will see that you're not your body because you're still there. There is consciousness, but the body is gone. Then you know that death is just a transition. It can happen in normal life without physical death. It simply means the loss of the physical attachment to the identity with the body. When you know that your identity is not the body then a new level of the void emerges, the black emptiness. Each level of dissolution brings in different experiences of the void, different grades of space.

When the attachment to the body is understood, all the attachments begin to dissolve; you know that it is not you. You know you would exist without it. The need for the attachment is gone. Then there is not the fear and desire that will lead to the attachment to that particular body, to that particular level of identification. When the attachment to the body is understood, and you go through the death experience, you know you are not any of these things, images or sensations, and you see the true identity of Essence, the true self. This is death and rebirth. You are aware of your true identity.

Then the next level of the void needs to arise, the level of the dissolution of identity. We need to see that the attachment to identity itself is also hell and frustration. At this point you begin to see hell more clearly and feel it more palpably. You start burning. The more attached you are to that identity, the more you feel the burning and frustration. Then the dissolution of self, or the dissolution of identity, is what we call extinction, annihilation, or nonexistence, which is a new level of the void. Not only your body is gone, but also your identity, your ego, is gone.

After ego extinction there is cosmic identity or cosmic consciousness. Now the identity, the ego, is gone, but there might still be attachment. We have dissolved the roots of attachment, fear, and desire but the process of attachment itself, the actual activity of attachment can exist without a center. You can have a very subtle attachment to the cosmic identity. It doesn't even feel like attachment. You can experience God, but as long as you want only that there is still some preference, some attachment. Now the identity is seen as the cosmic ocean, but there remains some identity, though it's not personal. On the personality or Essential levels there is no identity, but the cosmic identity is still there.

Now there is need of another level of the void to eliminate the final attachment, and we need to do nothing but see and understand this attachment to the wonderful cosmic existence, the all powerful, our truest nature. It is your truest nature, but the issue of attachment is not whether the object you want is good or bad, but that the movement of attachment itself creates separation and suffering. As on all the levels we have described, nothing needs to be done or can be done except to understand. True understanding will spontaneously bring in the deeper level of the void, which is complete, utter emptiness. There is no question of attachment to anything because there is literally nothing to be attached to, there is nothing. There is no image, no body image, no body, no personality, no Essence, no God, no existence, no nothing.

It's hard to visualize what this means; in fact, many of the things I say are hard to imagine. The issue here is not what you are attached to. What is needed now is to understand the attitude of attachment itself, regardless of object, even if there is nothing to attach to. Attachment can exist at the level of the cosmic existence as a remnant of personality, although the identity with the personality is gone. Reality exists in two poles, existence and non-existence. The fullness that is love and the complete, utter emptiness or nothingness are just the two poles of reality. Attachment to any of these is attachment. So the final attachment that must be resolved is the attachment to either existence or non-existence—God or nothing.

This resolution results in the big void, which eliminates identity itself—small or big, true or not true. There is no identity, nothing to identify. There is no object whatsoever, even a boundless object. This big void, or complete nothingness, is most necessary for freedom because it eliminates attachment. It is the freedom beyond which there is no freedom. Of course, with that freedom, there will come everything. Everything will be freed—the cosmic consciousness, the guidance, the true identity, the Personal Essence—all Essence in its various aspects will be there with no one experiencing it. It's just there.

To summarize, this process is a matter of investigating your identity, at any level of identification, and your attachments to it. That's why one of the most powerful techniques in spiritual traditions is to ask yourself, "Who am I?" and to keep asking. Every time you say, "That's me," investigate and continue asking, "Who am I?" until there is no one left to say it. It's not a matter of trying to push or do something. There's no need to do anything at all; all you need to do is understand what's there. The moment you want to do anything, your motivation is attachment. The awareness of exactly what's there, whatever it is, without wanting or not wanting, is finally the void, the final freedom.

The Phenomenology of Space

For most people the first sign that space is manifesting is the awareness of some definite sensation on the top of the head. It feels like a gentle tingling, or sometimes, as if something is brushing against one's hair. If the person is ready for the experience, it will develop into more intense sensations at the top of the head which can sometimes feel painful. This will develop into the distinct physical impression of the presence of a hole on the top of the head, as if part of the cranium is missing. This is usually a gentle and pleasant impression, quite distinct and unmistakable.

Lara is a woman in her mid-thirties, married with children, and at this time she is talking to me in a Work group setting. We are discussing her belief that it is bad or objectionable for her to be happy and joyful in a childlike, playful manner. I am aware that she is at the moment experiencing a lot of joy and delight, but she is reporting painful feelings. As she explores her defensive image of the suffering woman, she becomes aware of the joy she is actually feeling; she feels it pervading her chest. At this point she starts becoming aware of a tingling sensation at the top of her head. By focusing on it, she becomes aware of a specific impression of a hole or opening on the top of her head around the anterior fontanel. I don't pursue this experience with her, partially because she is just experiencing a new expansion (joy), and partially because I know she has many fears about losing her sense of identity, fears that go along with a defensive stubbornness in thinking furiously and being in her head.

What is actually happening in the experience of the hole is that the individual consciousness is in tune with the dimension of space in that area of the head. Since space is experienced as nothingness, there is the impression of a hole in the cranium, as if the top of the head has been surgically removed. This is not a hallucination; it is an actual accurate perception of the subtle dimension of space localized in that area.

A person who is more sensitive will then be aware that the hole is really a part of a column of space which starts at the cranium and goes upward into the space above. This perception is good evidence that the space we are discussing is not the common physical space, since it can be differentiated from physical space by a fine perceptual capacity. Also, more refined perception can sense the onset of the experience of space as a descent of a column of empty space above the head. When it impinges on the cranium, the individual has an impression of a hole.

This experience, if the person is not too frightened and is ready for it, will automatically develop as the perception of a column of space extending downward in the head. Now the person will be aware of it more definitively as an empty space, instead of as a hole. The mind is experienced as clear, empty, and lucid.

It can happen also by a descent from above of a great spiritual stillness imposing silence on the mind and heart and the life stimuli and the physical reflexes.

The column of space can descend all the way down into the body, encompassing the spinal column. This can cause shaking in the spine or in the rest of the body due to resistances against the presence of space. It can also cause disturbances in body balance, for it will affect the inner ear if any physical contractions are present in the ocular segment of the body armor.

Mark is a young professional man in his thirties, present in a Work group setting. Several students have been discussing the experience of a hole in their genital region. He tells me with some apprehension that he is afraid that he too has a hole in the genital area. From private sessions that I have done with him, I know that he has intense castration anxiety. I explore his experience of a hole in the lower part of his body by asking questions. Instantly, he starts becoming aware of a column of space inside his head. Here he experiences his mind as empty, clear, and with no thoughts. He feels, without any anxiety, that he has no physical boundaries around his cranium. He not only has a hole, the entire cranium is missing in his awareness.

This is a common action of space. It erases even the sense of body boundaries. The loss of physical boundaries is experienced as a lack of separation between inside and outside. It is also felt as pleasant, freeing, and unburdening.

Gradually, Mark becomes aware of all of himself as empty, pure nothingness, a void, a space. The column of space expands until his whole sense of himself is a lightness, an emptiness, a spaciousness. Mark mentions that he has no emotions. He experiences himself as a witness, a passive and silent witness. There

The Diamond Approach

is only space, and the space is aware, or the space is the awareness itself.

Here we see another dimension of space—the openness is also in the dimension of awareness. In fact, it is aware space. It is as though there is pure and open awareness at each point of the emptiness. This is what gives the sense of mental clarity, lucidity, and precision in such an experience.

In Mark's experience, space continued to expand until he felt himself as having no physical boundaries, with the space extending to infinity. Here then is the direct perception that the nature of the mind is really boundless space.

Besides directly sensing, intuiting, and being space, he could also see it. He could see it as emptiness, just like empty, physical space, but clear and immaculate. This is one of the common ways of seeing the inner space—as a clear and empty nothingness, the way we would imagine totally empty physical space. With eyes open, the physical environment is seen as it is, but with the more subtle perception of space pervading everything and extending infinitely.

It seems that Mark's sense of a hole in his genital region was actually the experience of the lower part of the column of space. At first he was aware only of the hole in the genital region because his attention was drawn to that area due to the focus of discussion in the group.

The experience of the lower part of the column of space is also connected to the experience of a genital hole. More accurately, the perception of the presence of a physical cavity develops into the experience of empty space only if the individual does not resist perception of the cavity and the emotions accompanying it. However, most people report the emptiness as a darkness, as a dark and empty hole, which engenders fear in them. If the individual does not resist the perception of the dark and empty cavity, it will expand upward to include the entire pelvic area, the belly, and the rest of the body. So the perception of space will extend upward in this case.

We should note that the qualities of space as perceived in these cases vary. Space is seen, for example, as clear or dark emptiness. The clear emptiness sometimes looks shiny. The space becomes a shining or glimmering void. More accurately described, it attains or becomes translucent, as if seen through cellophane. This happens either as a result of greater perceptual sensitivity or as a result of a deepening of the presence of space. Even the dark space can shine sometimes. It becomes a luminous blackness, as if the blackness has brilliancy. This feeling is similar to the experience of the peaceful and spacious darkness of the night. There is space and absolute stillness.

Martin is a professional married man, in this session confronting some marital difficulties. He talks about the possibility of separating from his wife. Here he gets a bronchial reaction, a difficulty in breathing. He feels fear of suffocation. He then remembers feeling this way as a baby; this makes him feel yearning for his mother. But he then experiences a rigidity in his body, as if there is a solid film spreading all over his body. By staying quiet for a while and breathing gently, he feels the solid film slowly melting. The experience of space arises in him, and he is able to allow it to develop. Soon, it becomes fluid, alive, and golden. He experiences an intense happiness, a pleasurable melting.

Our main interest here, however, is not in the pleasurable, golden merged state but in space and its connection to merging. The fact that, in some cases, the emptiness of space leads into a fulfilling golden fullness (or any other specific state) gives us a glimpse of the further uses of space, of the creative aspect of space. The golden fullness is not the only fruit of the creativity of space. The creativity of space is unlimited.

In fact, the experience of space itself can develop and deepen into a higher form of space, a space that is neither empty nor full. It is a dimension of space where the physical boundaries of the body are not erased by emptiness, but experienced as space itself. In this case, space simultaneously holds two opposites: emptiness and fullness. It feels empty and light, but also feels full and has density. Space here is not an absence, but a presence. This is unfamiliar for the ordinary mind. However, this unfamiliarity is only a boundary that can be dissolved, or in this case, itself seen as a space. This phenomenon is known in Buddhism and referred to as the unity of emptiness and form. The *Prajna-Paramita Sutra* says: "Form is empty, emptiness is form; form is no other than emptiness, emptiness is no other than form" (Chögyam Trungpa, *Cutting Through Spiritual Materialism*, Boston: Shambhala Publications, p. 188).

◆

CHAPTER 5

ESSENCE

THE EXPERIENCE OF the human Essence is central in the Diamond Approach. Ali calls Essence "an actual and palpable ontological presence" and points out references to it in many of the spiritual traditions. Loosely speaking, it is the human spirit. Essence is always present, but we usually fail to recognize it as such, or we experience it only in mediated, dampened ways. For instance, when we feel tenderness and caring for a friend who is suffering, the Essential quality of Compassion is arising. However, when we are identified with our personality structures, we may experience this Compassion through emotions such as pity or sorrow or through our thoughts as a kind of logical deduction about our feelings.

The experience of Essence itself, on the other hand, is direct and immediate. There is nothing between us and our experience. This immediacy and presence of Essence is deeply moving. By learning to recognize Essence, we learn to live at a depth unknown to most people. This depth of Essence is the source of an enormous richness. It is also the basis for genuine responses to the world rather than conditioned or constricted reactions. Essence cannot be adequately described in words, but the experience of Essence is unmistakable.

In his books, especially *Essence,* Ali goes into greater detail in discussing what Essence is not (mental images, insights, emotions, bodily sensations, intuition, or personality) as well as what it is. Concepts from psychological and spiritual traditions (including concepts from Sufism, Buddhism, Hinduism, and Taoism) are closer to Essence. It is related to the notion of energy as it is sometimes used in Hinduism (the chakra system), in Sufism (the Lataif, or subtle centers), and in Reichian and bioenergetic psychology.

A handful of psychological theories have also pointed to the true nature of human being. Abraham Maslow's peak experiences and Being-needs, Carl Jung's archetypes, and Karen Horney's "true self" come closer to Essence. However, none of these concepts expresses the full depth and richness of Essence.

The content of mystical experiences and spiritual emergence, the Buddhist notion of Basic Goodness, the "vision" of vision quests, Heidegger's notion of releasement—all of these refer to experiences of Essence. When Rumi writes about "the Friend" or "the Beloved," when Kabir writes about "the Guest," or when Lao-tzu writes about "Tao," they are pointing to and expressing Essence. Although Essence is not identical or interchangeable with these other concepts, it is pointing to the same true nature. Furthermore, the range of these references to Essence gives a clue to the many ways it can manifest in experience.

It is also closely related to descriptions of a subtle or spiritual substance. Essence is, in fact, often experienced as a substance with texture, density, color, taste, sound, and the like. However, it is not a physical substance, and so it would be a mistake to equate Essence with physical energy or substance. Initially, this subtle energy or substance seems secretive and esoteric. However, Essence is not intrinsically hard to experience. It is not so mysterious; it is just difficult to recognize through the veils of our personality structures. Once it is experienced and recognized, it becomes easier and easier to see it as our very nature, omnipresent and underlying all existence.

Because the personality is usually the focus or reference point of our experience, Essence may seem to come from outside. This can give Essential experiences a sense of grace, as if they were being bestowed. In fact, since Essence is more fundamental and intrinsic than the personality, it is merely outside our usual frame of reference. However, the distinction between inside and outside misses the point when your experience is open to the unfoldment of Being. It is possible to have a very deep sense of the personal nature of Being without identifying with the personality, personal history, or object relations. In fact, the reactivity and constriction of the personality and identification with the conditioned structures of personal history block Essence.

Essence is our basic nature, and most of its aspects are available in full and complete form to each of us. Even in the infant—perhaps especially here—these aspects are present. However, the soul needs to develop and mature in order to experience these aspects fully and in an integrated way. The structure of the infant's soul is very open but primitive. Aspects of Essence arise within the child as they are needed. If these aspects are fully experienced, they are integrated and enrich the soul. If they are blocked or constricted, they are experienced in only a limited way, according to the personality's defensive structures.

As the soul is freed from its defensive veils and as it develops, Essential aspects become more accessible and integrated. Although these Essential aspects themselves do not change, with development and maturity, they become realized in your soul or consciousness. Essence, as your basic nature or spirit, is always present, but the realization and accessibility of Essence is not. Full realization of Essence is possible only after

The Diamond Approach

extensive life experience and psychospiritual development. A particular aspect of Essence, the *Personal Essence,* is central to this process of integration and development (see Chapter 7).

ASPECTS OF ESSENCE

On the personal level, Essence has precise qualities or aspects. Each aspect is a unique differentiated quality, and each has specific psychological issues associated with it. One of the most important contributions of the Diamond Approach is the discrimination and description of Essential aspects, along with their psychodynamic obstacles, in language appropriate to our time.

Here are some very brief descriptions of some Essential qualities to give you a flavor of this realm. Most of us have experienced a warm, sweet, melting quality, perhaps focused in the heart. Ali calls this quality the *Merging Gold Essence.* The quality can feel like warm golden honey in the sun, a rich, sweet, satiated, and fulfilled quality. You may observe it in an infant who has just finished nursing, or you may have felt it just after making love. Merging Gold can bring a deep relaxation and a blending and merging of energies, as if you and your lover were part of the same sweetness. The Merging Gold Essence is not the result of these conditions, although these conditions can open many people up to this kind of quality.

The *Strength* or *Red* aspect of Essence is characterized by experiences of vitality, capacity, and expansion. (The color of each aspect is often a good descriptive shorthand. Thus, the Merging aspect of Essence is called "the Merging Gold" and the Strength aspect is called "the Red.") It is the source of energy that initiates action and is the means through which Being asserts itself. This aspect is the source of the courage to encounter difficulties and the drive to pursue our lives. It can feel to many people like anger, but it is actually a passionate aggression in the service of the truth of your Being. We recognize this Red in an infant who is hungry and makes its need known in no uncertain terms!

Essential Compassion usually arises in the presence of suffering or hurt, either our own or others'. It is a tenderness, kindness, and warmth. The Compassion Essence is experienced as green. It may be a rich emerald green or a fresh, light green. Like other qualities of Essence, it may be experienced as a subtle vapor or green-tinted space, as a liquid with depth and fluidity, or as a solid emerald or green diamond. Each of these textures still feels tender and kind. It is sensitive to, and even appreciative of, suffering. When we see another suffering and we are able to withhold any fear-based impulse to rush in and help or run away, we may feel this kind of openhearted response arise. Essential Compassion is not the same as pity, sympathy, or reactivity; it doesn't seek to take away hurt as much as it allows us to see, tolerate, and penetrate our hurt. Thus, Essential Compassion serves truth and understanding, the ultimate resolution to suffering. This truth, then, is the source of real and appropriate action. Essential Compassion opens the door to acceptance, action (fueled by the Red Essence), or simply being present with the hurt.

Each aspect of Essence manifests in a particular way when it is blocked. Then we experience an imitation or "false" quality of Essence. For instance, blocked Compassion manifests as issues with hurt (either an oversensitivity to hurt or dulled, blocked feelings of hurt). False Compassion feels like pity or a demanding need for relief of pain rather than genuine tolerance of suffering and the ability to see into it. When we lose touch with the Strength Essence, it manifests as issues of weakness or anger, depending on whether the Red is merely blocked or a compensation is developed. False Strength, then, is an aggressive or hostile imitation of Essential Strength.

These issues block awareness and integration of these Essential aspects and are resolved by these same aspects. Avoiding hurt blocks compassion. Clinging to or rejecting anger blocks Essential Strength. When these reactions are explored deeply enough, the experience of Essential Strength resolves the issues related to weakness. The next chapter will explore the relationships between the true and false qualities of Essence.

Ali has described and taught his students about many of these different aspects of Essence. Each aspect has precise qualities and specific roles to play in the work of becoming a complete and fulfilled human being.

The following two excerpts give a sense of Essence. They point to the fundamental place of Essence in our lives and our development and to some of the ways in which Essence can be misunderstood and blocked. They also suggest the central importance of the understanding of Essence in the Diamond Approach.

Essence

It is true that Essence is a substance, but it is not an inert substance. It is a substance that in itself is life, awareness, existence. Take clear water, for example. Imagine that this water is self-aware, that each molecule is aware of itself and of its own energy and excitation. Imagine now that you are this aware substance, the water. This is close to an experience of Essential substance. Of course, this is hard to imagine for someone who does not know Essence. And the Essential experience is much more than this. Essence is not alive; it is aliveness. It is not aware; it is awareness. It does not have the quality of existence; it is existence. It is not loving; it is love. It is not joyful; it is joy. It is not true; it is truth.

The quality of aliveness of Essence is of a different order from that of the body. The body is alive, but Essence is life itself. Essence is like packed, condensed, concentrated, completely pure life. It is 100 percent life. It is like a substance in which each atom is packed with live existence. Here, life and existence are not concepts, not ideas or abstract descriptions; rather, they are the most alive, most intimate, richest, deepest, most moving, and most touching stirrings within us. The experience of Essential substance can have such a depth, such a richness, such a realness, such a meaningfulness, and such an impact on our minds that some people actually get dizzy, unable to take the impact directly.

It is not experienced as something alien, distant, or neutral, like a physical object or an idea. No, we experience it as that which is most intimately ourselves. It is most deeply our nature, and it is the most precious and most beautiful center of us. It is our significance, our meaning, our nature, our identity. It is what moves our hearts, illuminates our minds, fulfills our lives. It is so near a thing to our hearts that only the heart can taste it. It is so near a thing to us that it is actually the very substance of our identity. It is so significant a thing for us that it is the only true nutrient for our life. It is the reality of us, the truth of us. It is the very substance of truth and the innermost secret of all truths. It is the most precious thing in existence.

Essential substance is so beautiful and magnificent that no imagination can conceive of its beauty, and no poetry can convey its magnificence. The way it moves us and teaches us is beyond the wildest dreams and imaginations of humanity. Its potentialities are staggering, its creativity is boundless, its depth is endless, and its intelligence is limitless. It is a wonder—a wonder beyond all miracles. It is our true nature, our most intimate identity.

This wonder is not just for stories or poetry. It is not just to dream about or long for. It is not just to give us flashes of its magnificence, or fleeting tastes of its significance. It is actually our human Essence. It is who we are: our very beingness. We are to be this Essence, to exist and live as Essence. It is our potential to be our Essence, not just in occasional experiences but always and permanently. It is our Essence that can and should be what lives, and what should be the center of our life. It can and should be inseparable from us. The work of inner development is not aimed only at having an experience of Essence. It is aimed at the complete realization of Essence and the permanent existence of us as Essence. It is aimed at the eradication of our separation from Essence. To be free is simply to be. And to be is simply to live as Essence. In fact, when we are not consciously Essence, we are not existing. The life of the personality is nonexistence, a wasted and useless life. There is life only when there is existence, and existence is Essence.

To be a genuine human being, a complete human being, is to be Essence. To be Essence is then not just an inner experience, but a total experience—a complete life. Life is then the life of Essence both inner and outer, in the privacy of our hearts and in the shared experience with others. Essence is then what dictates our actions, what determines our way of life, and what shapes our environment. This is real harmony.

Essence Is the Life

Essence is the promise. Essence is the life. Essence is the fulfillment of all our deeper longings. Essence is the answer to all our fundamental questions, absolutely—with no exceptions. This is such a fundamental point, but at the same time, such a difficult point to understand. When you understand it, it is even more difficult for you to accept. Usually, when you first come here, you are interested in getting something, or in getting rid of something—to get this or get rid of that. That's fine. However, in time, by using the understanding of the Work, you will see that most of your suffering comes exactly from that attitude. And that is what has to change. This Work is not for you to get this or to get rid of that. What you have to change is something much more fundamental. It's another part of you that has to start functioning, not that part of you that wants to get or get rid of something, regardless of what it is you want to get or get rid of. If you go deeply into yourself to understand your mind and your Being and the suffering in your situation, you'll find out ultimately that there is no fulfillment but to be, to be yourself, to be your Essence. That to be is to be free. That to be is to be fulfilled. That to be is to enjoy. Everything else, if it is valued more, will be a hindrance to your fulfillment and satisfaction. As I said, it is very hard to accept. And because Essence is the fulfillment and satisfaction which is what everybody wants, what everyone longs for, we call this work "Ridhwan." There is no exact translation in English for "Ridhwan," but it is close in meaning to "satisfied," "fulfilled," "contented." *Ridhwan* is a verbal noun in Arabic which not only means "satisfied," "fulfilled," "contented," but also means "satisfying," "fulfilling," "making content." It conveys a quality and an action. Ridhwan is Being that acts, acts by its very being.

Usually, our preoccupations are misdirected; they are preoccupations of the personality, which bring us suffering. We believe that if we get what we want, what the personality wants, we will be fulfilled. But fulfillment is ultimately the freedom from desires. So what I am saying is that being oneself, being one's Essence, free from the desires of the personality, is the fulfillment. It's not that you want your Essence so you can get something else. It's not that you want your Essence so that you'll get rich or fall in love and live happily ever after. It's not that your Essence will enable you to have children, or do special things, or be famous. If this is your attitude, the dissatisfaction and the suffering will continue, because you are not seeing where fulfillment lies.

It's a very tricky business, this one. The reason it's tricky is that the perception of Essence can come very close to the perception of certain emotional states. As many of you know, Essence is not an emotional state; it's not an emotion. Essence is Being, is something that is actually, substantially there. Most of you fail to understand the significance of that point, of what it means for Essence to be there. Because you fail to understand the significance of that, you tend to confuse Essence with emotional states.

When we experience Essence, we tend not to value our Essence as much as it deserves. We do this for many reasons. One reason particular to this work here is that it is easy to get it. In a year or two of working here, you start experiencing your Essence, which throughout history has been purported to be very, very difficult to achieve. So when you get it in this easier way, you tend not to value it. The culture we live in is materialistic. The more you pay, the better the thing is that you bought. If you get something without paying a lot, you don't think it's worth much. It works the same way with your true nature. Because it is easy to get, a lot of the time you don't see the significance or the value of it; you don't realize that without Essence, there is nothing. Without Essence there is only suffering.

There is another more universal and general reason why we don't value our Essence. We talk here about how much of your suffering, how much of your conditioning, resulted from the lack of love in your environment. Your environment wasn't support-ive, wasn't loving, did not respond to you appropriately accord-ing to your needs, did not see your value. That is true. But we don't see the fundamental thing that happened. The fundamen-tal thing that happened, and the greatest calamity, is not that there was no love or support. The greater calamity, which was caused by that first calamity, is that you lost the connection to your Essence. That is much more important than whether your mother or father loved you or not. You lost your own love be-cause of that. Because your value wasn't seen, wasn't responded to, you lost your connection with your own value. Because your joy was responded to with hostility or judgment or disapproval, you had to cut it off, and you lost it. And now we believe we will have it if we get that approval. "I will have value if somebody sees the value in me." We lost it because no one saw it.

But we've seen that what matters is experiencing it, and why should we care whether someone else approves or not? If your Essence is going to depend on the approval or perception of other people, then it is not free. We look at what happened in our childhood, so that we can see how we lost our Essence, so that we can retrieve it. But if we continue believing that we have to get what we haven't gotten from the outside, we will continue to do what we have done all our lives! And this is what caused our misery and suffering. So we think because our environment wasn't hospitable, wasn't compassionate, wasn't loving, wasn't supportive, we think we can get satisfaction by getting an environment that is loving, compassionate, perceptive, and appreciative of who we are. And what we are saying is that we want that positive merging again, otherwise we're not going to feel good. "I have to have somebody who loves me. I have to have somebody who sees me, who values me." It is true that it is useful and supportive at the beginning, but if you continue depending on it, this will stop you from owning and being who you are. Being who you are, being your Essence, should be completely independent of any other factor, inner or outer.

As I said in the beginning, Essence is the life, is the fulfillment. It's not the environment, not the situation, not the job, whatever. It is Essence itself, your Essence.

There is also another reason why when we start perceiving and understanding our Essence, we start seeing it in other places where it doesn't exist, and we tend to idealize and admire situations or people who don't have what we believe they have. The reason is that when our Essence is lost in childhood, when our parents don't see our value, don't value us for just being there—when this happens, our own value is lost, the Essential aspect of pure, absolute value is gone. And as we know, a deficiency results, a nothingness, a hole in the place of that loss. When an Essential quality is cut off, the result is what we call a hole, a deficiency, a lack. And we attempt to fill that hole, that deficiency, by trying to get value from the outside, instead of seeing that the value was ours to start with, that we were just cut off from it.

But there is an even more difficult complication, which is that one way to fill the hole is to make a false value, to pretend to yourself that you have value when you don't feel you really do, because to feel the absence of value, its lack, is too painful. So most people tend to create false Essence to cover up their feeling of lack. What the personality consists of is false qualities of Essence. We call the personality the "false pearl." Each person retains the memory of what was lost and will try to imitate it, will try to act, believe and feel in ways that are so close to the Essential qualities that after a while the person fools himself, and other people as well. Some people do this more than others, and some people are better at it than others. The personality is really nothing but an impostor trying to take the place of Essence. And these false qualities of Essence, what we call the crystallization of personality, are what we see in most of the people around us who are called successful. Everyone else believes they've got it made. They appear to have genuine qualities of confidence, compassion, self-assurance, self-esteem—but for the most part, these are false qualities. Just as these people have convinced themselves that these false qualities are real, they convince almost everyone else as well.

As we begin to get in touch again with our own Essential qualities, and the experience is new to us, we are innocent, or naive. For instance, when we begin to feel our own value and see false value outside in the world somewhere, we tend to believe real value is there. When I begin to experience love, and I see false merging love in other people, I tend to think, "Oh, that person's got it too, isn't that wonderful?" This is when objective perception is needed to see what is actually there, not to be fooled by the personality, especially because we have all kinds of unconscious reasons to want to believe this person has it, this situation has it, or a certain group has it, or a particular ideology has it. It is so hard for us to feel that we ourselves actually have it. We think, "If I'm the only one around who's got it, I'll end up all alone." Yes, you might. All alone and happy. That's a choice that each one of us is going to have to make. This doesn't necessarily mean that you will have to be alone, but it does mean that you have to make the choice of being willing to be absolutely alone, if that's what it takes to own your Essence. Eventually, you will be faced by this choice: Do you want to be "loved" and "appreciated" and "seen" and miserable? Or do you want to be "alone," "uncared for," "everyone thinks you're terrible," and happy, genuinely happy, at the same time? That's a choice everyone will have to make. That is the true independence, the true realization of Essence, that your Essence is not dependent on your exterior life at all. The whole world might be against you, but if you are your Essential self, you will be content.

As long as you hold onto wanting something from the outside, you'll be dissatisfied, because there's a part of you that you are still not totally owning. How can you be complete and fulfilled when there's a part of yourself you are not owning? How can you be complete and fulfilled if you believe that you can't own this part until somebody else does something, or the right condition arises? If it's conditional, it's not totally yours.

What we're doing here is fundamental. We're not playing a little game of getting a little something here, a little something there. There's no real resolution, no real fulfillment, until a person is totally committed to the Work, and can face being alone. Essence is the answer. You have to see that and accept it completely. Nothing else will do. No half measures. All the way. Absolutely all the way. You're going to be alone, and you have to be willing to be alone. Essence transcends life and death. After a while, when you start realizing what your Essence is about, even if you are threatened with death, so what? Who cares? Die, live—what's the difference? And you know that if other people don't like you, it's fine. It's all the same to you. You're not going to change yourself to suit anyone else's ideas of how you should be. In fact, you can't have any real intimacy until you can tolerate your own aloneness, integrity, individuality. That is freedom.

◆

CHAPTER 6

THE THEORY OF HOLES: ABANDONING AND RECOVERING ESSENCE

LTHOUGH ESSENCE IS OUR TRUE NATURE, we live virtually all of our lives out of touch with it. If Essence is intrinsic, how does it happen that we do not live from that place? This question is at the heart of spiritual work. For in understanding how we abandon our true nature, Essence, we discover a path for retrieving and developing it. The Diamond Approach uses the insights of depth psychology and spiritual wisdom to understand how Essence is blocked and recovered. These insights also form the basis for the Diamond Approach's path for reconnecting with our Essence. Ali calls this explanation the *Theory of Holes*.

ABANDONMENT OF ESSENCE

In the beginning of your life, your soul is pure and open. Essential states arise as they are needed. For instance, the Strength or Red Essence came when, as an infant, you needed food, and the Merging Gold Essence came when your needs were fulfilled in a satisfying way. Of course, you didn't know or understand these experiences. Neither were they integrated into your soul in a mature way. They simply arose in a natural and spontaneous way.

However, as you develop, interactions with the world are imprinted on the soul. The earliest experiences will be a mix of support and nonsupport. Support allows the unfolding and development of the soul in a way that is open to Essence. The Essential states that arise begin to be integrated into the soul, and the soul develops accordingly. Nonsupport, in the form of abandonment or punishment, constricts the soul's flow and arrests its development. Insults or wounds to your Being cause pain, and the natural instinct is to close off to that pain. Pain occurs whenever you are not held in the broader sense of being accurately mirrored or when there is active suppression or rejection. This can occur when parents are out of touch with some aspect of their own being and get defensive when that aspect is present in you. Defenses develop to protect you from the pain of rejection and abandonment. These defenses produce patterns or structures in the soul, and the soul begins to rigidify.

Consequently, aspects of Essence are gradually lost to consciousness and the functioning of the soul. The various intrinsic qualities of our Being are split off. As this happens, we lose both awareness of these qualities and access to them. Of course, Essence itself is always present in the infant and in the adult, whether it is experienced or not. Although we sometimes refers to the "loss" of Essence, the Theory of Holes is actually referring to the loss of the experience of Essence. Essence is not lost; it is abandoned. In adults, this abandonment is *experienced* as a hole or an emptiness, both psychologically and energetically.

If the Essential aspect of Will is blocked, you may experience anxiety or lack of support. This experience may also be felt as a hole or an emptiness in your solar plexus, the energetic center related to Essential Will. If Essential Compassion is blocked, the hole may feel like an emptiness in your heart and a lack of kindness either toward yourself or toward others. The hole of Essential Strength can result in a feeling of weakness, lack of capacity, or an absence of vigor and passion.

These holes are painful, so painful that we develop ways of removing them from awareness in order to function in our lives. The consequences of this attempt to protect ourselves from pain and anxiety are enormous. The complex psychodynamics involved in splitting painful experiences from pleasurable ones are a central cause of the development of personality structures. The development of these defensive personality structures coexists with other, less defensive and more functional structures. Yet much of the personality structure serves to (1) defend against painful experiences and (2) compensate for lost qualities of Being. The resulting personality or ego is defensive and inauthentic, out of touch with its nature. It is rooted in a sense of deficient emptiness and separation from its source.

As I have said, a soul separated from Essence develops structures and defenses to compensate for the lost aspects of Essence. These compensations mimic the qualities of Essence, but they are ultimately rooted in a defensive avoidance. For instance, out of touch with Essential Will, you may develop a stubborn or willful exterior in order to avoid the anxiety of feeling no support or confidence. This false Will is a defense against the hole of Will and, at the same time, a substitute for genuine will or the capacity to persevere in the service of the truth and to live according to Essence in the face of challenges. Out of touch with authentic Compassion, you may experience the hole of Compassion as hurt and attempt to "fix" the hurt by becoming loving in a desperate and solicitous way. This false Compassion serves as a defense against the underlying feelings of hurt or cruelty and as a substitute for genuine Compassion. Compensation for the hole of Strength includes identification with passivity and weakness or aggression. Identifying with these compensations and fake qualities constitutes the basis of the shell of the personality. At the same time, because they are imitations of Essence, they can help us find the genuine qualities of Essence.

The shell's experience is based on mental images of self and other from the past. The structuring gives it a sense of rigidity, compulsivity, fixation, and stuckness. When this structure breaks down, it is common to experience emptiness. This emptiness usually feels like the lack of a particular quality, such as Strength, Love, Will, Peace, yet it can also feel like a general and nonspecific deficiency.

There is a tendency in spiritual circles to judge the ego as bad. While seeing ego as a source of suffering and a false substitute for your true nature, the Diamond Approach also recognizes a wisdom in the ego. The ego is, in a sense, the best we could do in the difficult situation of a childhood that did not recognize our Essence. The ego developed in part to provide the necessary support and holding for survival and growth. Thus, it is not the ego per se that is problematic, but the identification with it. More important, the ego serves as a pointer to Essence. Because the ego exists as an attempt to replace or compensate for the loss of Essence, there is a close correspondence between ego and Essence. The qualities of the shell imitate Essence. By exploring a particular experience of the ego-shell, the issues underlying it are revealed, and the quality of Essence that had been lost is recovered. The personality is thus a gateway as well as an obstacle. Ego points to the life of Essence.

RECOVERY OF ESSENCE

Once you understand the condition of being out of touch with Being, two things need to happen.

First, the ego structures need to be softened, melted, and seen through so that Being can be more fully experienced. These ego structures are defenses against feeling the wounds of having abandoned Essence. Exposing the defenses allows us to experience the underlying wounds or holes. Since the real wounds are the abandonment of Essence, experiencing them reveals Essence. The ego structures and defenses block Essence; by working through them, we experience the holes themselves. Thus, we recover the Essence that was blocked. This is the work of *self-realization*.

Second, these same aspects of Being that were repressed need to be integrated into your life and allowed to mature. This is the work of *self-development*. Since Essence is not really lost, the recovery of Essence is a process of opening into what is deeper in your nature. Relating to the childhood wounds makes it seem as if you were "going back" to recover something that was lost. Instead, the recovery of Essence is a matter of realizing its presence and influence here and now and integrating it into your soul. Essence is the ground under your feet, always there but forgotten, longing for you as you long for it.

Individual work on the recovery of Essence includes three broad steps. Basically, they retrace the steps involved in the loss of the experience of Being. In the first step, you become aware of a pattern of compulsive emotions, behaviors, and thoughts. This may be felt as a continuing hurt, difficulty, wound, compulsion, or inauthenticity in your life. These states stem from the nature of the ego as conditioned, compulsive, reactive, and stuck. The second step explores these issues more deeply, often with the use of awareness and mindfulness practices, bodywork, and the guidance and support of a teacher. The ego-shell begins to soften or dissolve. Here, you contact the emptiness or deficiency that lies at the root of the emotional issues or compulsive behavior. This deficiency is the lack of Essence and, if experienced deeply, leads to an experience of space. Space indicates the melting or deconstruction of some part of the personality structure. If you stay with the experience of space, the third step occurs, the manifestation of Essence. Essence may initially be felt as a presence. This presence may be accompanied by a sense that the experience is authentic, real, clear, and more genuine than ordinary emotional experiences.

The particular aspect or quality of Essence that manifests depends on your needs in a particular situation. Since the issues stem from the lack of a particular aspect of Essence, the resolution of the issue will be the presence of that aspect. For example, if your issues stem from a block to Essential Strength, you will usually experience first your anger, hostility, or frustration, followed by the hole of strength: weakness, constriction, and a defensive passivity. This will be followed by space and then Essential Strength: energy, expansion, vitality, and the awareness of strength itself. This kind of open and sincere exploration of your experience (the first step) is common in psychotherapy and personal growth work. It naturally leads to the experience of space. However, many of these explorations stop here with the discharge or release of the difficulties that brought you to therapy. The relative freedom from issues and wounds is taken as the end point. In the Diamond Approach, this is just the beginning. This space is the opening that allows a deeper exploration and integration of Essence.

To summarize, the experience of Being is abandoned, lost to consciousness, or suppressed when Essence is rejected by the child's environment. This loss leaves a hole. The ego attempts to defend against this hole by blocking it from awareness, filling it with a compensatory quality or behavior pattern. These compensations form important parts of the personality structure. Those interested in realizing their full potential can use this knowledge in recovering Essence. Exploring a difficult issue or an unsatisfactory experience thoroughly can lead to an experience of the absence of Essence, a hole. Exploring this hole leads first to a sense of emptiness and then to an experience of space. The experience of space, in turn, allows for an aspect of Essence to manifest. The particular aspect of Essence that manifests is the specific aspect that was missing from the hole.

In the first passage here, Ali applies the Theory of Holes to the loss and recovery of Essence using the Essential aspect of Value as an example. This passage also illuminates some of the connections between the Diamond Approach as a spiritual path and the knowledge and practice of psychotherapy. In the second passage, he reminds us that our work on our holes is not merely to overcome our sense of deficiency and suffering. The purpose of working with our holes is to realize Essence, and it is always and only Essence that fulfills us.

The Theory of Holes

In all the history and literature of the Work, we see that knowledge of what we are here calling "Essence" is what could be called the goal of the Work. In Western philosophy we find Plato talking about pure ideas, or the Platonic forms. Plato, a student of Socrates (who was doing the Work), wrote about Socrates' discussions with his students concerning what are called the "eternal verities"—what we call here the qualities of Essence, such as courage, truth, humility, love—and he wanted to show how people learn about these things. Socrates finally demonstrates that we can't learn these things from anyone else. No one can teach you, for instance, the quality of courage, or the quality of love. He showed in his final arguments that we can know these things only by remembering them.

Everyone has some memory of these Essential forms. We have seen in our work here that a consistent characteristic of the experience of the Essential states is the feeling that you have known it before, you have been here before, you are recalling a somehow more fundamental reality which in the process of living your life you have forgotten. So we know that although we are generally unaware of it, this memory of Essence exists and we know that the process of remembering our Essence is the process of remembering ourselves, of returning to our true nature.

Another thing we need to know in order to understand how our method works is that Essence is not one big lump, not one state or experience or mode of being. It is not ESSENCE, one big thing. Essence has, or is, many states or qualities. There is truth; there is love; there is compassion; there is objective consciousness; there is value; there is will; there is strength; there is joy. All these are Essence, in different qualities. They are different facets of the diamond, reflecting different colors.

Although it has always been known in the Work that Essence has many facets, most schools have emphasized one quality or cluster of qualities more than others. Some schools, for instance, emphasize love. So they use techniques to develop love. They talk about love. They pray. They chant. They worship the guru. They worship God. They "surrender" to love.

Other approaches emphasize service, work. They use the belly centers more. Others emphasize truth, or the search for truth. Others, Gurdjieff, for example, emphasize will—making supreme efforts.

Which aspects of Essence are emphasized by a given method depends on the experience and character of the teacher, or the originator of the method. Often, for instance, a teacher will have had to work through a certain part of himself or herself more deeply than other parts. Then the quality of Essence associated with that part may be very strong; and since it is through that quality that the teacher reached the understanding and embodiment of his or her Essence, the method of teaching develops around that quality.

Only a very few schools have existed which work with the totality of Essence. So there is apparent discord between the different teachings: Mohammed speaks very differently from Jesus, and the Buddha tells it his way. Present teachers say different things—some say surrender to God; some look for the "blue pearl"; some say to make a conscious effort, to look for your will; some say the answer is the Void. And since most of these people don't know that Essence has many qualities, each thinks the others are wrong. If you know, or feel, that great efforts of will are leading you to your Essence, it seems obvious to you that love will not work. Love might imply to you weakness, sentimentality. So we see in some groups, for a time at least, will is developed actually at the cost of the quality of love because they appear somehow incompatible.

We know that Essence is something we learn about by somehow remembering it, and that it has many different qualities. You have all had direct experience of these things. So when and why did we forget that which we are now working to remember? Everyone is born with Essence, and as you grow, your physical body develops and your Essence also develops, according to a certain pattern.

The newborn baby is mainly in the state we call the Essence of the Essence, a non-differentiated state of unity. At about three months, the baby is in a "merged" state, which is necessary for the development of the relationship with the mother. After the merged state, strength develops, then value, joy, the Personal Essence, and so on. But, of course, because of interference from and conflict with the environment, this development is only partial. Every time there is pain or trauma, there is a lessening of a certain quality of Essence. Which quality is affected depends on the nature and the time of the trauma. Sometimes our strength, sometimes our love, sometimes our self-valuing, or compassion, or joy, or intuition, are hurt, and then eventually blocked.

When a quality of Essence is finally blocked from a person's experience, what is left in place of that quality is a sense of emptiness, a deficiency, a hole, as we saw in our discussion of the Theory of Holes. You have seen in your work here how you actually experience that emptiness as a hole in your body where a quality of Essence is being cut off. So there is created in a person the sense that something is lacking, and therefore, something is wrong. When we feel such a deficiency, we try to fill the hole we feel in ourselves. Because the Essence has been cut off in that place, we cannot fill the hole with Essence. So we try to fill it with similar, false qualities, or we try to fill it from the outside.

Suppose, for instance, that our love for our mother is rejected, not valued. Then that love in us is hurt, wounded. To avoid experiencing the hurt, we deaden a certain part of our body, and in that way we are cut off from that sweet quality of love in ourselves. Where that love should be, we have an emptiness, a hole. What we do then, to get that love which we feel lacking, is to try to get it from outside ourselves. We want someone to love us, so that hole inside will be filled with love. We know exactly what we want, but we forget that it was our love that was lost; we think that we lost something from outside, so we try to get it back from outside.

Connected with the "hole" are the memories of the situations that brought the hurt, and of the quality that was lost. It is all there, but repressed. We do not remember what happened or what we lost; we are left simply with a sense of emptiness, and with the false quality or idea with which we are trying to fill it. In time, these "holes" accumulate, and as they are filled by various emotions and beliefs, the material filling them becomes the content of our identity, our personality. We think we are those things. And the personality is structured around the strongest deficiencies. Some people are left with a bit of Essence here and there, and in some whose childhood problems were severe, everything is repressed, resulting in a subjective sense and a look of dullness, almost deadness.

It is this knowledge which makes the work we do here, the Diamond Approach, possible. Now we are able to be very clear, very precise. We have an obvious way to lead people back to themselves. You learn first to sense yourself, to pay attention to yourself, so that the necessary information is available to you. Most people go through life without this self-awareness because they are trying to avoid feeling the emptiness, the falseness, the sense that something is wrong with their lives. So you learn to be aware of yourself, and you begin to look at your personality.

What makes it possible to do this? The things that can empower your work are: whatever will you've got, and whatever love and understanding for yourself you have. You must have some openness, conscious or not, to your desire to return to your true nature. In addition, you must have some understanding that your difficulties come from inside you, from your own conflicts. If you fundamentally believe that your problems will be solved by making more money, becoming more beautiful, having children, getting a better car, and so on, you cannot do the Work. The work begins by seeing that the difficulties come from inside us, and sensing that the fulfillment we are seeking will also come from inside.

Then, we use various forms of the old techniques, such as meditations, to strengthen different parts of the Essence. We also use various psychological techniques to understand the blocks against the issues around the different aspects of Essence. We see in our work here that each person can observe in himself certain clusters of behaviors around a given issue at any particular time in his life. If you continue to work on those things, you will observe that you're behaving in those ways to fill a certain deficiency or "hole." By now, we are beginning to see which of the different qualities of Essence are generally related to which kinds of issues from one's past. These relations between the Essential state, the "hole" or specific sense of emptiness which resulted from the loss of that state, and the emotions and beliefs we create to fill those holes, and finally the conflicts in our lives which arise from the resulting false personality, are all understood. These relationships and patterns are the same for every human being. So when a person is working here in the group, I can tell by what issue he is working on, which Essential state and which deficiency are involved.

For instance, the loss of the will is generally related to fears about castration, as we discussed earlier. The loss of strength is related to repression of anger and also fear of separation from mother. The loss of compassion is always due to suppression of hurt. Each "hole" is filled generally by the same thing, with variations depending on the childhood history, and the cultural and social circumstances of the person. Compassion, for instance, might be replaced by sentimentality and belief that you are a loving person; intuition might be replaced by excessive ideation, and strength by a show of being tough.

If you deal thoroughly with the set of issues related to a given state, if you reveal an aspect of the false personality as an attempt to fill a hole, if you go all the way into that sense of emptiness, through the fear of feeling it—all the way—you will get to that quality which has been lost to you. We have seen this over and over again in our work here.

Psychotherapists deal with the issues, but in general they go back only as far as the deficiency, by seeing the original issues and understanding or resolving them. They don't see that the emptiness is there because of lack of Essence. They see only the sense of emptiness and the conflicts which result from the childhood history.

Sometimes, I'm sure, clients in therapy get to Essential states. But the usual therapist doesn't see it, and the client herself won't perceive it as significant. She will only know that she feels wonderful, relieved; she will sometimes even have a strong sense of having "come home to herself." But the Essential state will not be recognized for what it is; the experience will be ignored by the therapist and lost by the client, never pursued or developed.

But when you are working with a person who knows that it is possible to go through the experience of loss, all the way back to that which was lost, and who recognizes these Essential qualities, then seeing and developing your true nature is possible. We are not interested here in just going back through your childhood, understanding your conditioning and your conflicts. We are interested in going back to the original "hole" and simply experiencing it without trying to fill it. In therapy, if you deal with the conflict that you wanted your father and your father was emotionally unavailable to you, you feel deep hurt and you feel castrated. You see that you can't get your father in the present, so the resolution is that you relate to another man (sometimes the therapist himself) to fill those "holes," and this is the therapeutic resolution.

It doesn't work. You can try to fill the deficiency of the loss of love with the love of another man. But since it is your own love, your own will, for which you ultimately long, you will feel dissatisfied with the love and support from the father substitute, whoever it is you are using to fill the deficiency.

You know now that you can experience your own love, or your own will, only by allowing yourself to experience the "holes," the deficiencies associated with them, instead of trying to fill them. This is very difficult and frightening. A lot of spiritual disciplines use techniques to enable students to stay with these things. But when you finally can do it, the real resolution happens, the resolution not of simply resolving the emotional conflict but of retrieving the lost quality. The presence in you of the quality of love will finally eliminate the problem of love for you. The presence of will is what will eliminate the sense of castration, or powerlessness. Nothing else will do.

And you have seen that you can begin with any emotions, thoughts, difficulties in this work, and work through them, right to the original deficiency. By staying with this process, following each issue all the way, you will finally have the memory of what you lost, as Socrates said. And by remembering it, you will have it. Everything you have lost you can regain by working like this. Everything.

There is no separation between psychological issues and Essence; they are intertwined, woven together. This is why you cannot just set to work eliminating the false personality and, when that's done and taken care of, start experiencing and developing Essence. Without the retrieval of that which personality was created to replace, personality simply cannot be dissolved.

The reason the Diamond Approach can be precise is that we know that each aspect of Essence is connected with certain psychological/emotional conflicts. So we can use the powerful psychological techniques which lead us to perceiving and understanding our conflicts, repression, resistances, and patterns of resistance, and just become conscious of these things. We don't need to push against the resistances, the dark spots, we simply shed light on them. After a while, they disintegrate. Then the passage is easy. We can flow through those places rather than having to go around them. Going around them or pushing through them is the hard way, the long way. Our way has more to do with understanding, with the precise diamond clarity.

Essence Is the Teacher

Essence is a relentless teacher. It does not stop at any aspect. After one aspect is understood and realized, it starts manifesting another aspect. This aspect in its turn now pushes into consciousness the particular sector of the personality connected to it, and makes it imperative for us to understand and resolve it. The emerging aspect makes us feel the lack of its quality. It makes us long and yearn for it. Gently but consistently, intelligently and knowingly, it puts pressure on us to start longing for it. Then it provides us with the insights, the intuitive knowledge that helps us understand our disharmony. And finally it shows itself, culminating our experience by manifesting itself as a complete and absolute resolution for our conflicts.

Essence is then the teacher. Essence is then the taught. Essence is then the freedom. Essence is then the realization. Essence is then the fulfillment. Essence is then the being. Essence is then the very nature and substance of the individual. Essence is then the experience, the experienced and the experiencer. Essence is then the truth. Essence is then the nature of all reality.

This process of Essential development continues as personality is clarified and worked through. Essence manifests itself to the individual's consciousness as the true strength, will, joy, compassion, love, peace, truth, fulfillment, consciousness, awareness, knowledge, freedom, samadhi—as one aspect follows another. The amazing richness of Essence manifests in that there is an Essential aspect for every important human situation or condition, the aspect that is experienced as the complete and exact fulfillment for these situations. The exactness, the precision and fitness are astounding. The beauty of Essential action cannot but fill the consciousness with wonderment.

There is for instance, an aspect that relates to pleasure, and this is different from the aspect of joy, which is different from the aspect of fulfillment, which is different from the aspect of satisfaction, and so on. There is the aspect of personal will which is different from the universal or divine will. Then there is the aspect of Essential Conscience which guides your lifestyle and manner of relating to others. There are aspects that lead to the harmony of your environment. There is an aspect that acts as a protector of the Essential life which is different from the aspect of the defender of Essence. There are aspects that relate to love and its various manifestations. There is a light, fluffy love, compassionate love, merging love, passionate love, divine love, and so on. The richness and the beauty of Essence are endless. And the beautiful thing is that this richness acts at the same time to resolve personal conflicts and disharmonies.

The personality slowly loses its grip. The conditioning is gradually shaken loose, and the ego is exposed in its bankruptcy. Finally, the aspect of death manifests, and then the ego-identification starts dissolving. This marks the entrance into the divine realm of Essence, where grace and mercy begin descending into consciousness, dissolving more and more of the ego boundaries. This ultimately leads to the understanding of enlightenment, and the emergence of the Supreme aspect. There is even an aspect that has to do with the search and with the end of seeking.

This in turn brings about the manifestation of the magnificence, the majesty, the exquisiteness, the magic, and the beauty of Essence. Now, ego does not need to be slain. You do not have to wage war against ego, conquer, or destroy it. Ego cannot but shatter at the recognition of the sheer beauty of Essence and all of existence. It cannot but melt in the experience of the overwhelming precision and delicacy of Essence. It cannot but bow and surrender at beholding the magnificence and majesty of reality.

Essence—the teacher, the tempter—becomes ultimately the very stuff of our consciousness, the very substance of our beingness, the beauty of all existence.

No wonder that Essence is called the agent of inner transformation, the elixir of enlightenment. The elixir is the hope, it is the solution, and it is the fulfillment.

◆

CHAPTER 7

THE PERSONAL ESSENCE:
THE PEARL BEYOND PRICE

Both psychological and spiritual teachings are concerned with the nature, purpose, and role of the personal self. Psychodynamic approaches promote the development of an integrated, stable, coherent, and enduring ego and see pathology as stemming from the failure to develop a healthy ego (or personality structure). Cognitive psychologists might describe a similar goal as an integrated and realistic self-schema. On the other hand, spiritual systems generally emphasize the need to transcend this sense of self. From the point of view of most spiritual perspectives, suffering results (at least in part) from identifying with the ego.

Some transpersonal psychologists suggest a sequential view. The ego must be first developed and then transcended as you move developmentally from personal to transpersonal levels of personality development. This view is expressed in the aphorism "You must be somebody to become nobody." This is accurate in the sense that the permanent transcendence of ego requires a stable ego structure and an integrated, coherent sense of self. However, if this is misunderstood, it can seem that spiritual awakening requires the loss of being your own person. Then, being personal and autonomous seems to run counter to spiritual realization. After becoming somebody and then nobody, a new question arises: How can you be yourself while being nobody?

THE PEARL

There would appear to be a contradiction between our impersonal Beingness ("the nobody") and our personal autonomy ("the somebody"). The Diamond Approach resolves this contradiction by recognizing an aspect of Essence called *the Personal Essence, the Pearl beyond Price,* or simply *the Pearl.* The Pearl has the qualities of autonomy, beingness, personalness, and contact. It is the embodiment of independence, authenticity, and integration of all your aspects. Your ability to live in the world in satisfying and fulfilling ways and to have genuine personal contact with others is rooted in the Pearl, but its origin is Essential, spiritual, and unconditioned rather than historical and conditioned. The Pearl is often experienced as having a soft, round fullness, pearly-colored and luminescent, with a feeling of authenticity and wholeness.

The Pearl is the embodiment of "being in the world but not of it" in that it supports functioning from an authentic place rather than through the object relations of the ego. The characteristics of such functioning include the capacity to learn and grow, delay gratification, integrate experiences, be spontaneous, and maintain healthy, authentic, intimate relationships. Some psychological concepts have come close to this notion. They include Horney's use of "true self" and the use of "being" by Winnicott and Guntrip. It seems that these theorists approached the Pearl but did not have the means or conceptual framework to explore it directly.

PERSONALITY AND THE PEARL

Since each aspect or pattern of the ego is an imitation or a counterfeit of Essence, they point to qualities of Essence. For example, stubbornness imitates Essential Will, anger imitates Essential Strength, and pity imitates Essential Compassion. The personality is a substitute for and counterfeit of an Essential aspect, the Pearl.

The ego develops in response to situations in the world in order to support functioning, foster integration, create stability, delay gratification, promote self-respect, and provide a sense of personal dignity and worth. Over time and through healthy interactions with other people and the world, the ego structure develops and its functions mature. However, a healthy ego is not the end of development. As the self develops, the ego is no longer the foundation of our experience. Some would say it is transcended. However, the ego characteristics are not abandoned in self-transcendence but emerge in a more full and integrated way in the Pearl. As a refinement of ego development, the Pearl embodies the functional characteristics of the ego in a way that is authentic, open, and flowing. It is the true personality.

As we explore our identifications with our conditioned personality, we may come to experience the false Pearl. This is the totality of our sense of individuality, autonomy, and personalness that is based on defenses and attachments. It is based on a fear of loss or an avoidance of suffering, as is true for all the false qualities of Essence. In this case, the fear may be the fear of not being real, not being ourselves, or of losing our identifications and attachments. (Yet we remember that who we really are is Essence, not our attachments.) Experiencing the false Pearl directly, we may sense a kind of thickness and stickiness in our experience rather than the light, flowing quality of Essence.

Since the false Pearl or personality is rooted in the belief that we are our attachments and identifications, the fear of losing them is a deep and difficult issue. It will arise again and again in our deeper spiritual journey. However, seeing through the false Pearl is necessary for manifesting Essence in a personal and integrated way in our lives. And since the false Pearl imitates the Personal Essence, it, too, can guide us to the truth.

DEVELOPMENT OF THE PEARL

As the Pearl develops, the ego structures are integrated or metabolized into the self, and you mature in a personal, integrated, and well-rounded way. The Diamond Approach suggests that the ego is not so much transcended as it is metabolized. However, most of the time, such metabolism is blocked or is at best only partial. Experiences that are not integrated give rise to ego structures. Identification with these ego structures forms a counterfeit of the Pearl. This false identification is a source of suffering.

The Pearl develops as experience is digested. At the same time, the more developed it is, the more experience can be digested without the need to form the defensive, rigid structures of the ego. In a sense, the ego and the Pearl are parallel developments, one inauthentic and one authentic, rather than strictly sequential steps. Ideally, as the ego develops, it is metabolized into the Pearl. When, because of psychological barriers, the Pearl's development is stunted, the ego develops without being integrated into Being. Later, when the Pearl is recovered, the old, not-yet-metabolized experiences and the psychological structures built around them must be integrated. Thus, the Pearl grows and develops.

The Pearl is the only Essential aspect that does develop. This is in contrast to other Essential aspects, which are whole and complete in themselves. For example, an infant may experience the Merging Gold Essence when it is nursing and being held in a positive and loving way, feeling satisfied, contented, and melted into a union with the mother. As adults, we can experience this same Essential quality. The infant's Merging Gold is just as real as the adult's, but the adult's ability to experience, recognize, integrate, and function with this kind of love is qualitatively different from an infant's. The infant does not yet have the capacity to experience the Pearl. An adult may, if the Pearl has developed sufficiently.

Furthermore, as the Pearl develops, the adult's experience of one aspect of Essence can be integrated with other Essential states. This functioning may be evident, for example, in the integration of the Strength Essence with the Merging Gold. Remember that some of the qualities of the Strength Essence are assertion and passionate aggression. The Pearl brings the capacity to relate to others with an integration of this assertion and a melting union. We can sometimes find a place that holds both the energy of the Strength Essence and the melting of the Merging Gold without compromising either one. What to our usual ego may have seemed contradictory—assertion and merging—is a natural capacity of the Pearl.

The understanding of the Pearl helps to resolve the question of whether spiritual realization is a matter of recovering Essence or of developing it. The Diamond Approach answers that both are true. Most aspects of Essence are lost and need to be recovered; the Pearl, however, must develop. Thus, Ali's understanding of the Pearl shows how psychological development is an aspect of spiritual development. Psychological development is part of the development of the Personal Essence.

ESSENCE AND HUMAN DEVELOPMENT

Essential aspects may be recovered and integrated at different rates. Some aspects of Being can become highly developed in a person, while other aspects are relatively undeveloped. Thus, development can become "lopsided." This can be understood by understanding the factors in a person's developmental history that supported some aspects of Essence and not others. This is true for all of us to some extent.

Some of us are very clear and present on matters of love, compassion, generosity, and caregiving, for example, but have difficulty standing up for ourselves and our own needs. One explanation of this is that we are highly realized in the Essential aspect of Compassion but not Essential Strength and Will. Thus, it is difficult for us to see and direct loving impulses or to direct the energy of love where it is needed most, including toward ourselves. Or we may be highly developed in many aspects, but in spite of this development, there remain blocks in the Joy aspect. In this case, we may seem clear and present but joyless and somber. The Pearl ensures and enables a more complete, well-balanced, and integrated development.

The work of self-realization requires commitment and understanding. As the nature and reactivity of the ego are understood and experienced deeply, and especially as issues related to authenticity and autonomy are seen and worked through, the Pearl develops and comes into consciousness more and more. You become more autonomous with a clearer sense of your uniqueness, preciousness, and dignity. As self-realization continues, the Pearl becomes more deeply integrated, first with other personal aspects of Essence, then with the universal aspects of Essence, and finally with the Boundless dimensions. This understanding of the Personal Essence, its development, and its blocks is one of the outstanding and original contributions of the Diamond Approach.

In these excerpts, Ali introduces the Personal Essence. In the first selection, he identifies two orientations: a concern with personal fulfillment and a concern with spiritual liberation. Generally, these are contrasted, but he shows how the Personal Essence is the integration of these two perspectives. In this way, we can appreciate the wisdom behind seeking a life that is personally satisfying while following the spiritual insights on the full realization of our true nature. The second selection briefly states Ali's view of the relationship between ego development and spiritual transformation. The third selection touches on the development of the Personal Essence as the integration of Essential aspects and the importance of the

The Diamond Approach

Personal Essence in supporting a balanced perspective on spiritual growth.

Spirituality and Personalness

At a certain age, very early on in life, each one of us becomes aware of himself or herself as a walking, talking, thinking, feeling being—in short, as a living person. It is such a luminous discovery, but it quickly becomes dull with familiarity. Then we live our lives as if we now know what it is to be human, as if maturing were only a matter of becoming more of what we think we are already. The mystery is gone, and life becomes tedious and repetitive.

In the Diamond Approach we want to lift off the veil of familiarity. We want to inquire into the mystery of being a human being, a person. We want to explore the potential of being human. What is the extent of this potential? What is a truly mature and complete human being like? How will we experience ourselves and the world, and what kind of lives will we lead?

We begin our inquiry by contrasting two poles of human experience. At one end of the spectrum is the experience of what we will call "the man of the world," the individual who is busy living a personal life, trying to find personal fulfillment, working on strengthening and expanding himself. It is an accepted and approved concern for a human being, in most societies, to seek personal happiness, fulfillment, and autonomy, in the process of building a personal life, as long as it is not at the expense of others. This has become the dominant view of man in modern societies. The personal life is the core of most human activities; what is called a public life is still a personal life, related to the person, and lived for persons. In our exploration we will examine in a new light the conviction that living a personal life centered around the person is its own value and end.

Contrasted to the perspective of the man of the world is the view of what we will call "the man of spirit," which considers a higher spiritual reality to be the true and proper center of real human life. The most profound teachings regarding human nature, those of the most accomplished and liberated of human beings, of the founders of the major religions, spiritual movements and philosophical systems point clearly, unequivocally, and exclusively towards the life of selflessness, egolessness and surrender to a higher reality. One teacher after another, one great religion after another, one moral philosophy after another, extol the life of spirit—in which personal life is subordinated to a higher spiritual reality—as the highest and most refined, most fulfilled and only true life for man. Humanity is exhorted to move towards making the personal life be governed by spiritual values, and towards embracing the universal and impersonal truths, which are beyond self and personality.

Thus, the main difference between the perspective of the man of the world and that of the man of spirit is that the first considers the separate personal self to be the center of life, and personal life to be its own value and end, while the latter makes a higher reality to be the center of life, and believes that the personal life must be subordinated in relationship to such a higher reality.

As we see, the spiritual teachings of the mystical branches of Christianity, Judaism, Islam, Hinduism, Taoism, and Buddhism are unanimous in their evaluation of personal life as less important than some "higher" realm. What does this mean? Does it mean that the majority of humankind are completely astray, are so wrong and ignorant and completely out of touch with their nature that they go in the exact opposite direction from where they should be heading?

This is not to reject or devalue the truth of impersonality and universality. This truth remains the ultimate reality, the absolute nature of man and of all existence. Still, we are exploring human nature and human existence in order to understand human life in its true perspective. We put our inquiry so far in the form of a question: is it possible to understand ego and personality in a way that gives a meaning to the orientation of most of humankind, without contradicting the spiritual perspectives?

The perspective of most spiritual teachings is that ego is a falsehood, and hence it must die for there to be truth. We will show that this is true, but that it is not the whole truth. We will show that the ego, with its sense of self and personality, has a truth hidden within its nature, a truth that is not necessarily visible from the transcendent and impersonal state. We will show that ego is a reflection of a truth, an attempt to imitate an absolute and eternal reality. In fact, we will explore how ego is nothing but a failed or aborted attempt at a real development. We will show that ego is a reflection, an imperfect one indeed, but still a reflection of true reality, the reality of the true human being. We will see that by understanding ego, rather than transcending it, we can understand and actualize the reality of what it is to be a human being. Only through this understanding and realization can we see what human life is.

We will see that this truth that ego tries to emulate is what most people are seeking in their personal life, and that realizing this truth of what it is to be a human being is the aim of humanity.

Humanity is in a sense astray, but there is a pattern to this way of existence which, when understood, reveals the true nature of the human being. Only this understanding will heal the schism and resolve the contradiction between the personal life and the spiritual life. The true human being, what we will call the Personal Essence, is the resolution of the contradiction. It is the integration of both points of view.

An important consequence of the understanding of the Personal Essence is a new perception of the life led by most people, the perception of a spiritual truth or an Essential element in the heart of all ego strivings. This means that in fact most of humankind are not astray in the usual sense of the word, but are after something real and precious. The difficulty lies in the fact that they do not know how to find it.

The qualities of the Personal Essence are those of fullness, autonomy, competence, respect, dignity, integrity, excellence, maturity, harmony, and completeness, among others. There is very little knowledge and guidance in the modern world about how to develop into such a true human being. The result is that most of us settle for an imitation or an incomplete development, which is the personality of ego.

Understanding that ego is a reflection, or an imitation, of a true reality makes it possible to connect to this reality. One need not go the usual spiritual route of abandoning one's personal life and the values of that life, but rather one must look deeply into those values and explore the true reality that they are approximating.

The path of the Personal Essence not only brings about the development of the real human being, but also opens an easier way to the realization of the impersonal universal reality. The reason that realizing the life of the Personal Essence is a more accessible path for human beings than the realization of the absolute universal reality is that the ego is a reflection of the Personal Essence, and hence ego can be used as a stepping stone towards it. The reason the realization of the Personal Essence makes entrance into the universal and impersonal realms much easier is that these realms are part of the natural and spontaneous development of the Personal Essence.

The Personal Essence allows us to see the meaning and the potential of a fulfilled human and personal life, a life of truth, love, dignity, and harmony, which includes the usual human concerns of work, family, creativity, accomplishments, and enjoyments of all kinds.

The Pearl beyond Price is an exploration of the Personal Essence—its nature, and its relation to the ego and to the transcendent impersonal reality. Our method is the realization and development of the Personal Essence through the understanding of its reflection, ego. The presence of ego points to the reality of the Personal Essence, just as the existence of false gold indicates the existence of true gold.

Ego Development and Spiritual Transformation

The Personal Essence can be seen as the integration or absorption of personality into Being, as the synthesis of the man of the world and the man of spirit. However, it is more accurate to see it as the ultimate product of ego development. In other words, ego development and spiritual enlightenment are not two disjointed processes but parts of the same process. The understanding of the Personal Essence shows how they are linked. This point is a radical departure from the understanding of both traditional spiritual teachings and modern psychology. It unifies these two fields into one field, that of human nature and development.

The Personal Essence is the real person, the true individuality. It is what is meant to be realized in ego development. It is the actual goal and completion of this development. It is the real individuation. It is not on the ego level or the spiritual level; for it is neither and both. There is only one human individuation, and that is the realization of the Personal Essence.

In contrast, object relations theory, and developmental psychology in general, consider ego development a complete process on its own, and spiritual teachings consider ego development either as a wrong development, or as a development that should be superseded by spiritual development.

In our understanding it is more accurate, and certainly much more useful, to see ego development as an incomplete development. It is more correct, from our point of view, to consider ego development and spiritual transformation as forming one unified process of human evolution. A human being grows and develops by learning from experience. Difficulties can occur at any stage of this process, including getting "stuck" on the ego level.

The Pearl beyond Price

Some systems have formulated the Work in terms of developing something that is already there, or even developing something that is not even there. Other systems have made their formulations in the form of uncovering and bringing out the Essence that is already there and already formed but inaccessible to experience.

The systems of the first kind assume that Essence is not there to start with, or is there in a primitive and undeveloped form that needs refinement and evolution. The second kind of system assumes the human organism has everything in it, already formed and complete and only needing to be exposed. In most circumstances this difference leads to a divergence of methods and techniques.

Another way of formulating the issue is to see development and uncovering as two complementary aspects of inner work, to assume that both are true. In many respects, the process of the Diamond Approach appears as more of an uncovering. Essence is buried, and the work is to uncover it and make it conscious. It is just completely reowning what was there to start with but was lost. This process also leads to the purifying of the personality, usually called the refinement of the ego.

Even the process of uncovering that we have described is experienced as a development. Seeing it as uncovering is both a theoretical formulation of the situation and a method of dealing with it. Experientially, the substance of Essence is first discovered, then goes through a transformation. This transubstantiation is the development of Essence from one pure aspect to another, until the Essence is completed.

From our perspective, what is discovered and realized first depends more on what sectors of the personality the individual happens to be dealing with than on an innate order of the aspects of Essence. From this perspective, it is immaterial whether we look at the process as a development or an uncovering. They are equivalent formulations, provided the process is looked at experientially. Theoretically, from the perspective of an overall understanding, the process is, so far, a process of uncovering. Essence is lost, then it is retrieved.

However, seeing the process as a development applies more accurately to a certain aspect of Essence, an aspect that is in a sense more central or that occupies more of a central place in the process of inner realization. We should recall here that each part of the personality is an imitation of and a substitute for an aspect of Essence. The ego structure as a whole is a substitute for a central aspect of Essence, which has a central position similar to that of the ego.

This central aspect of Essence is what we call the Personal Essence; in Work literature it is usually called "the Pearl beyond Price." It is actually the true Essential personality. It is the person. It is experienced as oneself. When the individual finally perceives it, the contented expression often is "But this is me!" The sense is of oneself as a precious being. There is then a fullness, a completeness, and a contentment. It is as if the individual feels full and complete, realized. Nothing is lacking. No more search, no desire or wanting anything else. The person feels "Now I have myself. I am a complete individual. I am full. I am fullness. I am complete. I want nothing else."

It is the experience of being oneself and not a response or reaction to something. It is not being something for somebody. It is in a sense complete freedom, the freedom to be.

Many people talk about wanting to be themselves, to have their personal freedom. But usually people are referring to their personality. Being free to be your personality is not freedom, although it might seem so. In fact, it is the prison. But to be the Pearl beyond Price is truly to be, completely and finally, free to be yourself. Now we can experience "I am" and not be referring to our personalities.

The Pearl is the real, complete, balanced, and rounded personality that psychologists believe they are talking about when they are discussing the ego. We must remember that the ego is a structure, or a structured process, whereas the Pearl is Essence, which means the Pearl is an ontological presence. We call it the Personal Essence because among all the Essential aspects it alone is personal. It is experienced as having a personal flavor to it, in contradistinction to impersonal. All aspects of Essence, even love and kindness, are impersonal. But the Pearl is personal. And this is its miraculous quality, totally unexpected and unfathomable.

Some people interested in inner development try to become objective and impersonal, to move away from identifying with the personality. The personality is personal, and so the personal feeling is mistrusted and avoided. However, the Pearl beyond Price feels personal without being the personality. It has the capacity to make a personal contact with another human being and still be free, totally unconditioned, free from the past and its influences.

It is the most personally intimate aspect of yourself. We all recognize what it is when we first see it. Sometimes even the vaguest perception of it brings out the exclamation "but this feels like me, intimately me." And yet it is not selfish like the personality. The personality is based on deficiency, and this is the source of its selfishness. But the Pearl is based on true value and true fullness. In fact, it is itself fullness.

Unlike other aspects of Essence, this personal aspect (the Pearl) goes through a process of development, growth, and expansion. Here the concepts of development and growth can be seen in their true and literal meaning. This true personality of the being is born, fed, and nourished. It grows, expands, and develops in a very specific sense. It is really the development of Essence from being impersonal to being personal. Others might call it God becoming a human person, an individual. One way of understanding the various aspects of Essence is to see them as the differentiation of the source. From the undifferentiated source the differentiated aspects of Essence emerge and are realized. Then, there emerges a synthesis, a rounded personality that is Essential. This integration of all aspects of Essence into a new and personal synthesis is the Pearl beyond Price.

The process of the development of the Pearl is the gradual integration of all of the aspects of Essence into a new form, a new substance. When the Pearl is first born, it is usually not complete; it is the Essential child. It is born as a personal kernel. Then it integrates all of the aspects of Essence into its very substance by spontaneous synthesis, until it is all complete, forming a harmonious human being.

Ego psychologists consider the ego to have the functions of integration and synthesis. Its synthetic function is becoming recognized as central. We see in the Pearl the real and true integration. The Pearl not only synthesizes; it is the synthesis itself.

This perception of the precious Pearl as the complete synthesis of Essential aspects is of fundamental importance. It safeguards against imbalance in inner development, for the Pearl is the balance. It safeguards against prejudice and sectarianism, for it has everything in its very substance.

Some systems and teachings equilibrate themselves around the knowledge and realization of one particular Essential aspect or a cluster of Essential aspects. When there is no complete knowledge, it is possible through some rigorous disciplines to focus on and establish one or a few Essential aspects, to the exclusion of others. This will establish a true Essential presence, with the power and beauty of Essence, but that presence will be incomplete and unbalanced. This limited Essential development is also an effective way of avoiding having to deal with some conflict-laden sectors of the personality.

So it is obvious how differences arise between the different systems and teachings and how this can lead to prejudice and sectarianism. If only some Essential aspects are developed, then some sectors of the personality are not understood, which will bring about various kinds of distortions. This is a very tricky situation to discern, especially for the individual concerned. When we experience our Essence, when we see the truth, the reality, the power, and the beauty of it, it is difficult for us to realize when something is not right. The imbalance is usually explained and rationalized away by the building of a system or a teaching centered around the Essential aspect or aspects known.

The systems built around awareness, for instance, will not understand and might even oppose the systems built around the Merging Essence. Each believes he has the truth, and both actually have the truth. But neither has the whole truth. Another clear example is the apparent contradiction between the teachings built around emptiness and the teachings built around existence.

However, if the precious Pearl becomes the objective of the system, then there is an innate and built-in safeguard. To really develop and establish the Pearl, all sectors of the personality have to be explored and understood. For the Pearl to develop, all aspects of Essence have to be freed, which will expose all sectors of the personality. Freeing it and establishing its life enables it to displace the totality of the ego structure. Then there is balance, completeness, totality, harmony, fullness, and contentment. There is then no reason to oppose someone or to convert anyone. All inner compulsion will be gone, for the person is realized, and the realization is based on fullness, richness, and value. The individual is then a mature human being, a complete person.

The station of the Pearl beyond Price is so significant because it is not a matter of a state of consciousness or a state of being; it is rather the condition of the actualization of your realization in your life. Being becomes personal being, a complete human being living fully the life of objective truth.

♦

CHAPTER 8

SELF-REALIZATION AND ESSENTIAL IDENTITY: THE POINT

M OST PEOPLE ON A SPIRITUAL journey are sincerely motivated by a longing to know themselves, to find or
create a life with significance, and a desire to truly
be themselves. We seem to know that our souls want to realize
their own true nature in ways that are uniquely ours. Most of
the time, we take genuine pride in our accomplishments and
contributions to the world. Our work and our relationships
are generally satisfying. We appreciate the recognition we receive from our friends and colleagues. We feel we know and
like who we are.

However, we also come to find that these sources of fulfillment and meaning are temporary at best, and even fleeting
and painfully shallow. The same longing arises again and
again. We discover an underlying layer of self-consciousness,
self-deception, and manipulation of others, all in the service
of this same sense of positive self-worth. When we are not
recognized or valued, or when our sense of self crumbles, we
feel frustrated, hurt, angry, or empty. The teachings of virtually
all mystical and spiritual traditions echo this difficulty. The
identification with our achievements and the desire to stabilize

the cycle of fulfillment and dissatisfaction brings suffering. These traditions point out that by identifying with our sense of individuality, we cut ourselves off from the very source we seek. We are often reminded, with or without the insight of spiritual wisdom, just how fragile and needy our sense of self is.

Dissatisfied with struggle and temporary satisfaction, we seek a more stable and positive sense of self-worth and self-knowledge. We sense that some kind of spiritual self-realization might complete this journey.

Eventually, if we do enough serious work on ourselves, we can begin to experience various Essential states. We find a fulfillment and release we had only dreamed of before. Yet even these experiences are transitory and leave us longing for more. We try to hang on to them or find the formula for how to re-create them, but they are gone. The emphasis on having more Essential experiences becomes dissatisfying and empty. How do we come to identify with the fullness, purity, and flow of Being? How are we to know ourselves as Being itself? How does the Soul recognize itself as Essence? How do we honor the desire to be ourselves, to be seen and appreciated by others, and to gain a stable and healthy sense of self while at the same time surrendering ourselves to spirit?

ESSENTIAL IDENTITY

The answer to these questions, according to the Diamond Approach, lies in the struggle for identity. The ego identity is an imitation of the *Essential Self* or *Essential Identity*. Our ordinary sense of self and ego identity is a distorted and shallow reflection of our true identity and source. Once again we see that we can reclaim the real by looking deeply enough into the false. We find that our disconnection and suffering is the exact doorway into self-realization. At some point, a shift must be made from *having* Essence to *being* Essence. The center of our experience must shift from the ego (which has experiences of Essence) to Essence itself; Essence must become our identity.

This is the work on the Essential Identity or, as Ali calls it, the Point. The Point is Being experienced as our identity. There is a sense of focus and simplicity about our lives. We relax into an authentic sense of our uniqueness. This realization is less about a particular experience and more about our relationship to our experience. It is a matter of being at home with ourselves and having a sense of being fulfilled with whatever we experience. Essence shifts from being an external object to being the center.

The realization of the Essential Identity and the realization of the Personal Essence are two complementary and necessary developments in this work. The Pearl is the Essential capacity for integration and functioning. It is the actualization of Being in the sense that it brings Being into our lives in a way that we can express it in our actions, feelings, thoughts, and relationships. As the Pearl develops, we grow more expanded, more well-rounded, and our personality is gradually absorbed into our souls. The Point, as we will see, is the realization of our identity as Being. The realization of Being is a movement of focusing our identity from the surface to the depth of our true nature. From the view of the Pearl, we express Being; from the view of the Point, we are Being.

Narcissism and Barriers to Essential Identity

The understanding of Essential Identity is a good example of the contributions of the Diamond Approach to the integration of psychological knowledge and spiritual wisdom. In his book *The Point of Existence: Transformations of Narcissism in Self-Realization*, Ali goes into great detail showing the benefits of psychodynamic psychology and spiritual wisdom to each other. Here, I will briefly summarize some of his work on narcissism and its relation to the Point. Although psychologists usually discuss narcissism as a serious kind of pathology, Ali points out that more fundamentally, it is the core spiritual disorder. The understanding of pathological narcissism is an important contribution, yet it is only the extreme of what every ego feels, healthy or otherwise.

Narcissism results from the loss of the true self. Our intrinsic nature is an identification with Being. As infants and young children develop, Being begins to reveal itself, and this identification is elaborated and deepened. However, because the child is not yet aware that her or his identity is Essence, it needs to be supported by the child's caretakers. Psychoanalysts call this support mirroring, reflecting back to children their intrinsic beauty, worth, and love.

A particular need for mirroring emerges for the toddler around a year to a year and a half old. At this stage, children are full of confidence and energy, just learning to walk, climb, and navigate their world. They feel invincible, omnipotent, and special. However, in terms of their bodies, this feeling is not realistic. They are not able to tell that this feeling does not reflect the power of their bodies but the magnificence of their Essence. They need positive and realistic mirroring of this sense of grandeur in order to continue to develop and integrate it. They also need support for the inevitable fall from grace as they grow to realize that they are not so omnipotent after all. Without the necessary mirroring, they fail to develop the awareness of their connection to Being and their Essential Self.

The child identifies with what is mirrored, idealized, and rewarded and rejects what is not seen or what is punished. As the child's true nature as Essence is not seen, met, or responded to, it is forced into the background. The lack of attunement to the child's true nature, combined with the powerful forces of conditioning, creates a new identity based on the need for love and pleasure and the avoidance of abandonment and pain.

Closely related to the need for mirroring is the need for positive ideals to support the sense of identity. These idealized *self-objects* (as they are called by Heinz Kohut and other psychoanalysts) are necessary in the development of the ego. We create and then attach to these self-objects, which then provide external support to the ego. Self-objects may include our parents, our children, physical objects, concepts, or even spiritual teachers and schools. They help to reinforce our sense of positive identity. Without them, we begin to feel alone and insecure. When these idealizations are threatened or break apart, we feel a disappointment, a disorientation, a hurt, and an anger.

The lack of support for our identification with our true nature comes both from a lack of mirroring and from disruptions in idealized self-objects. It is the source of a wound to the soul called the "narcissistic wound." This wound is the gap between what we actually are, Essence, and what we take ourselves to be, ego.

The reaction to the narcissistic wound includes a deep sense of hatred and an intense desire to bring down, devalue, or harm the cause of the wound. We can recognize such narcissistic rage in our hurt, frustration, and jealousy when we feel hurt, rejected, abandoned, betrayed, belittled, or shamed. Underlying the narcissistic wound and rage is the narcissistic hole or the hole of the Self, the distance between Essence and the ego. A hole indicates that some aspect of Essence is missing. In this case, it is the Essential Self that has been abandoned or lost. In this hole, we feel alone, vulnerable, and helpless. This is referred to as "narcissistic emptiness." This emptiness brings the experience that life is without meaning or significance and that everything is pointless. Nothing seems real anymore, and we are left with neither ground nor center. Avoiding the narcissistic wound and its hurt, rage, and painful emptiness sets up much of our struggle and suffering as adults. Working with this wound is, at the same time, the basis of a crucial part of the practice of the Diamond Approach.

The central issue of narcissism is identification. We begin

life with the possibility of identifying with Being. However, because of a lack of attunement in our social environment and through the forces of conditioning, we come to identify with a false self or shell. We mistake the surface for the depth and our reactivity for presence. We look outside ourselves for worth, significance, and identity. This mistaken identification is the root of narcissism and the core of ego.

THE SHELL

Abandoning Being and compensating for its loss results in the development of what Ali calls the shell of the personality. A shell (in this sense) results from taking a part of reality, the surface, to be the whole. When we are identified with it, it feels familiar and even reassuring. However, as we are able to step back from it a bit, or when it cracks because of a disruption in our mirroring or idealizations, we realize the shell is fake, shallow, and without depth or substance. It is a pretense, and we begin to experience it as a facade. We see that one of its functions is to avoid shame, worthlessness, and insignificance.

The shell fixates the ego, which continues our separation from what we really are, reinforcing our identification with the false Self. We may experience it as a pervasive sense of effort. This effort is accompanied by other attempts of the ego to maintain itself: choice, desire, motivation, hope, preference, attachment, rejection, holding, grasping, trying, wanting. To the extent that these reflect the activity of the shell to avoid the narcissistic wound, they will only perpetuate the gap between our true nature and the ego.

As we experience the shell more deeply, we will begin to feel as if the rug had been pulled out from under us. We find no support, and we feel as if we were falling or sliding with nothing to hold on to. We are suspended in emptiness with no ground. As the facade of the ego identity dissolves, we feel disoriented, as if there were no self. We find ourselves feeling ineffective and helpless. What are we to do? Nothing. Any doing will only tighten the knot. If we grasp for meaning, we are separated further. If we try to move toward self-worth, we only feel emptier. Life becomes like a koan in which we can only surrender and trust. We can come to understand that this shell is still the soul, only with a limited and limiting identification. But like the trick handcuffs we played with as kids, the harder we try to pull away, the tighter the structure gets. The soul as a shell and its underlying wound, rage, and emptiness don't need to be rejected. It just needs to be seen, understood, and released from the images and misunderstandings and delusions that bind it.

The Diamond Approach shows how narcissistic issues arise throughout the spiritual journey, creating shells that are deeper than the personality. Narcissism is not limited to the ego, the ego's identifications with self-images, and the products of personal history. Dealing with narcissism is not an all-or-nothing resolution. Narcissistic issues appear at all levels of self-realization. As the false self is seen through, our identity shifts to Essence.

However, there is a danger here. If we become identified with a mental image of Essence, a false self is created, and we are still taking the surface for the totality. If we become attached to Essence, a new shell is formed. If we penetrate the identifications both with our personality and also with our images of Essence, we may discover identifications with our images of all of reality, all appearance, and all form. In these identifications, the entire universe becomes the shell.

The resolution to this "universal shell" can only occur at the deepest levels of self-realization. Some of these questions of narcissism in the more subtle levels of Being will be touched on in the next chapter, and Ali discusses them at length in his book on the Point. For now, it may be enough to remind ourselves to be prepared to deal with narcissism in a variety of forms and levels of self-realization.

With this inquiry into the shell, several things happen. We may notice that a kind of soft compassion arises, much as we would feel seeing a child struggling with a difficult but critical task. We may experience the arising of what Ali calls the Diamond Will, a steadfastness and sense of capacity that supports our Inquiry. This Diamond Will is more universal than the personal Essential Will. An experience of Black Space also arises, a deep, still kind of emptiness.

Eventually, the Point itself appears. It has been described as a brilliant star, a radiant point of light. The Point manifests in our awareness as a shooting star that is omnipresent. This radiant shooting star is everywhere at once, moving in every direction. It has no source, but rather feels like the source of all perception.

It is experienced as a sense of balance, completeness, simplicity, and purity. There is no longer any gap between our immediate experience, our identity, and our true nature. The Point also brings a simplicity into our awareness and our lives. There is no desire, no holding back, no reflection, no complication, no paradoxes, no struggle. Our souls gain a greater focus on Being and feel uncontaminated. We are able to drop our guard, and we can simply "be" without concern about anything, including Essence or self-realization.

The Point also brings about a realization of our uniqueness. Such uniqueness is not about doing our own thing or holding our own unique perspective, although these follow naturally and spontaneously. It is also not about rejecting any teaching, teacher, or influence. Rather, when we abide in our own true nature, we cannot help but manifest our own path and opportunities. At the same time, we find this unconditional uniqueness is not opposed to any genuine teaching. We can love and express a particular spiritual teaching even more when we are identified with our Essential Self. We each become unique embodiments and expressions of that teaching.

The student becomes the teaching, and the relationship between student and teacher feels inexpressibly tender and intimate.

Each time the Point arises, we are self-realized, and the more expansive the Point, the more deeply we realize our true nature. We no longer are an ego that has Essence. We are that Essence itself. We recognize ourselves as whatever Essential states or dimensions arise. If fullness arises, we know ourselves as fullness, not as a self that is experiencing the state of fullness. If compassion arises, we are not compassionate; we are compassion. We know ourselves as Being. We become the Point sensing and knowing itself. And this self-realization becomes the flow of Being, never static and never finished.

These two selections discuss the Point. The first one focuses on the relationship of Essential Identity to ego identity. In the Diamond Approach, these two are not simply contrasted. As with other counterfeits for Essence, ego identity imitates and reflects the characteristics of Essential Identity. The second selection emphasizes self-realization as the meaning of Essential Identity. This second selection follows the selection in Chapter 3 on the self and soul. I recommend that you reread that selection for the sake of continuity.

Identity

The most tenacious sector of the personality is the sense of identity, the sense of self, or what is called in depth psychology the ego identity. In ego psychology and object relations theory, a distinction is made between ego and ego identity. The ego is the overall process and structure. But the ego identity, the self, is the organizing center, the apex of the developmental process. It is the normal sense of identity that people have. It is what we ordinarily mean when we say "I." It is an identification tag designating the ego, which differentiates the individual psychologically from other people. It is responsible for the psychological boundaries of the individual.

This ego identity is usually what is referred to in spiritual and Work literature as the ego. It is the ego identity that, according to most systems, has to die for Essence to become master, for complete liberation. It is intimately related to self-image, because ego identity is a psychological image, or what is called in object relations theory a "representation." Object relations theory believes that the ego identity or self-representation develops gradually in the process of structuralization of the ego. The belief is that it does not exist at the beginning of life but develops through the processes of internalization and identification. But the question of where the sense of identity itself comes from never arises. Where does the mind learn that there is such a possibility of having an identity? And how does the mind know what it feels like to have one? We are not wondering here about what differentiates one identity from another; we are asking about what differentiates identity from other categories of experience. For example, what differentiates ego identity from the feeling of ego strength? Where does the sense, the feeling, the recognition of the category of identity come from?

This is a big gap in ego and self psychology that is not yet even formulated. To assume that the sense of identity develops gradually as the various self-representations coalesce does not really answer the question. What do they coalesce around, and why do they always coalesce into a very definite experiential sense, always a sense of identity? Where does the element accounting for the feeling of identity (self) come from? Also, the sense of identity is usually experientially very vague, never really isolated. The vagueness of psychoanalytical writings on this question does not mean it has to be vague; it means only that it is still vague in the minds of the authors.

This is understandable, for this sense of identity, like all other sectors of the personality, is an imitation of a certain specific aspect of Essence. Ego identity is an imitation of the identity of Essence, the true self. The Hindus call it the Atman.

The sense of identity of the personality exists because there is an unconscious memory of this true self. The personality's sense of identity develops through the loss of the true self. The child had it to start with, but its loss led to the development, through internalizations and identifications, of the ego sense of identity coalesced around the vague memory of the true identity. A self-representation is felt as relating to self because of this vague memory of self. This is the reason for the vagueness about identity in everybody's experience.

This true self, the spark of our life, the most alive and most brilliant aspect of Essence, is, so to speak, the source of all Essential aspects. It is like the star of Bethlehem, witnessing the birth of Essence. Many work systems, many teachings, aim all of their efforts toward finally beholding and realizing the true self, our source, the brilliant Point of it all. This true identity, this aspect of I-ness, is what Ramana Maharshi, for instance, wanted his disciples to reach when he exhorted them to contemplate the question Who am I?

To free this aspect means finally to shift the identity from the ego to the Essence. This is the most difficult part of the process. Even after Essence in its various aspects is uncovered and freed, we find that we still believe in our personalities. We still hold tenaciously to the personality. The Essence is present, but we still think of ourselves and very often act, if we are not paying attention, as if we are the personality. That is why the death of this identity is so strongly stressed by all true teachings. But obviously it cannot be a burning one for the individual until Essence is realized because our experience is mainly limited by the personality. In fact, until then, it is very difficult for us to understand or appreciate the issue of the death of the personality.

For this final shift to occur, the deepest aspects of the structure of the ego identity have to be understood. Here the deep experience of ego death happens. The experience of the annihilation of the personality deepens and becomes very profound. This is because the sense of self is very much related to the functioning of instincts and in particular to survival. In fact, the whole development of the personality is primarily for survival. To understand completely the deepest truth of the ego identity is to understand the necessity of the ego and its identity for the purposes of physical survival. This is a profound question, and answering it leads to a knowledge of the relationship between Essence, the personality, and the physical body.

To understand and become free from the self-concept is to become free from instincts, from biological programming and evolutionary conditioning. This is made possible by coming to understand the relationship of life and death to each other and to Essence. So to live the life of Essence, the identification with the personality must end, through the discovery and the realization of the true and brilliant self.

This does not mean, as some teachings have it, that the individual must experience the Essential Self all the time, that we must hold onto it as the most precious thing. Many systems of teaching focus on the true self, concentrate on it, identify with it, and glorify it. This will naturally bring attachment, and attachment is personality, even if it is attachment to the Essential Self.

What needs to happen is to free this aspect of Essence for it to become a station, to become permanently available, so that it is there when its mode of operation is needed. Therefore, all of the issues around identity and selfhood must be seen and understood, including the need for or attachment to identity. The true self exposes all misunderstanding and conflicts around identity and selfhood. Resolving the issues around the Essential Self eliminates all identification; or rather, identification becomes a free, conscious movement.

Self-Realization

In every soul there is an inherent drive toward truth, an inherent desire to feel fulfilled, real and free. Although many people are not able to pursue this desire effectively, the impetus toward the realization of the self is in all of us; it begins with the first stirrings of consciousness and continues throughout life whether or not we are directly aware of it. This impetus spontaneously emerges in consciousness as an important task for the psychologically and spiritually maturing human being. As maturity grows into wisdom in an optimally developing person, this task gains precedence over other tasks in life, progressively becoming the center that orients, supports and gives meaning to your life, ultimately encompassing all of your experience.

What Is Self-Realization?

What is the experience of the self when the process of self-realization is complete? What is the actual experience of self-realization? Although self-realization affects many aspects of our experience (including how we relate to others and to the world around us), its central element concerns the nature of our immediate subjective experience. The experience of full self-realization is radically different from the normal ego-bound state; thus, the descriptions in this book may seem alien to the reader. It will help to keep in mind that what we are describing here is the pure state of realization; there are, however, many partial awakenings and openings on the way to the complete experience.

In self-realization our experience of ourselves is a pure act of consciousness. We know ourselves by directly being ourselves. All self-images have been rendered transparent, and we no longer identify with any construct in the mind. There is no reactivity to past, present or future. There is no effort to be ourselves. There is no interference with our experience, no manipulation, no activity—inner or outer—involved with maintaining our identity; we simply are.

We are able to respond, feel, think, act—but from a purely spontaneous and authentic presence. We are not defensive, not judging ourselves, nor trying to live up to any standard. We may also be silent, empty, or spacious. We do not have to do anything to be ourselves. We are whole, one, undivided. It is not the wholeness of the harmony of parts, but the wholeness of singlehood. We are one. We are ourselves. We are being. We simply are.

In this experience there is no narcissism. We are at ease, spontaneously real, without psychological artifacts, pretensions, falsehoods. We are not constructed, not even by our own minds. Our experience of ourselves is totally direct and unmediated.

How Does the Common Experience of the Self Contrast with the Experience of Self-Realization?
Under normal circumstances we experience ourselves only partially. We do not experience ourselves as we are in ourselves, in our authentic reality or Essence. Instead, we experience ourselves through thick veils of ideas, ideals, beliefs, images, reactions, memories, desires, hopes, prejudices, attitudes, assumptions, positions, identifications, ego structures, labels and accumulated knowledge—in other words, through the influence of all of our past experiences. We literally experience ourselves through the past, through the totality of our personal past, instead of freshly, in the present moment.

Only when we have experienced another way of knowing ourselves is it possible to appreciate the enormous effect all this mental baggage has on our normal experience of ourselves. We see, then, that our awareness of ourselves has become so fragmented, so indirect, so burdened by mental accretions, that even what we take to be authenticity is only a reflection of a reflection of our innate and fundamental authenticity.

The mental images and attitudes that determine how we experience ourselves form the basis of a whole implicit world view. We also experience ourselves only indirectly, as a subject experiencing an object. We are aware of ourselves as an object like other objects, seeing ourselves in the world as one object among others. Even when you are aware of yourself as perceiver or subject, this perception is different from the direct sense of your facticity, from the fact of your existence. We still know ourselves through the veil of memory.

As indicated above, ordinarily it is impossible to appreciate the extent of the influence of past experience on our sense of ourselves without having some other form of experience as a referent. What gives us the opportunity to see this omnipresent influence is the direct experience of self-realization, which reveals to us the distance between knowing yourself and being yourself. The self is constrained by the subject-object dichotomy: one is a subject experiencing oneself as an object. In the conventional dimension of experience the most intimate way we can experience ourselves is through such self-reflective consciousness.

In self-realization we experience ourselves as presence, where presence is both Being and knowingness. Here, the cognitive act and being are the same experience. We realize that we are speaking of a level of experience that seems far removed from ordinary experience, and may seem too esoteric to be concerned with. However, thousands of perfectly ordinary people have achieved access to this dimension of understanding, either through religion, spiritual traditions, artistic endeavors, or other kinds of explorations. The Diamond Approach makes it clear how this level of insight can unfold simply through our maintaining a consistent and open inquiry into our true nature.

The reason we experience knowing and being as a single phenomenon is that presence is the presence of consciousness, pure consciousness more fundamental than the content of mind. Although we usually associate our consciousness with the act of being conscious of some object of perception, experiencing the direct truth and reality of our consciousness requires no object.

When we can finally be ourselves fully, we recognize ourselves as presence, and apprehend that this presence is nothing but the ontological reality of consciousness. We feel our presence as a medium, like a material medium, such as water or clear fluid.

This medium is homogeneous, unified, whole, and undivided, exactly like a body of water. This homogeneous medium is consciousness. The medium is conscious and aware of itself. It is not aware of itself by reflecting on itself, but by being itself. In other words, its very existence is the same as awareness of its existence. To continue the physical metaphor, it is as if the atoms of this medium are self-aware. Presence is aware of itself through self-pervasive consciousness, where this self-pervasive consciousness is the very substance or medium of the presence itself, not an element added to it.

From the perspective of self-realization, then, the soul is simply our consciousness, free from the occlusive veil of past experience. She can experience herself directly, without any intermediary. She is thus dispensing not only with the veil of past experience, but also with the self-reflective act. She experiences herself by simply being. She knows herself to be a presence, a self-aware medium in which the awareness is simply of presence itself. She is. She is presence, pure and simple. She is aware that she is presence because presence is indistinguishable from awareness.

What Does the Experience of Self-Realization Feel Like?

The experience of self-realization, of knowing yourself as self-pervasive consciousness, is felt experientially as an exquisite sense of intimacy. The self-existing consciousness experiences itself so immediately that it is completely intimate with its reality. The intimacy is complete because there is no mediation in the self's experience of itself. We feel an exquisite stillness, a peace beyond all description, and a complete sense of being truly ourselves. We are so totally ourselves that we feel directly intimate with every atom of our consciousness, completely intimate with and mixed with our true identity. The contentment is like settling down peacefully at home after eons of restless and agonized wandering. Clarity and peace combine as the feeling of exquisite, contented intimacy, which is totally independent of the particulars of our situation, beyond the conceptual confines of time and space. The peace and contentment do not come from accomplishing anything, nor are they a result of anything. They are part of the actual feeling of being truly ourselves. We are not only intimate with ourselves, but our very presence is intimacy.

♦

CHAPTER 9

TRUE NATURE AND THE
BOUNDLESS DIMENSIONS

THE DIMENSIONS OF BEING described so far (soul, ego, and Essence) are personal. The soul is the individual consciousness and the container for our unique experience of Being. The ego is the patterning of our individual consciousness based on reactions conditioned by the past. The construction of the ego in the developing child reinforces a sense of separateness from our true nature. Identification with the ego results from a loss of trust in our true nature and in reality. With the ego comes struggle, effort, isolation, and fixation on the past. As the various elements of the ego are seen through, understood, and penetrated, it becomes less opaque, and the qualities of our true nature become more available. Our emotions, feelings, thoughts, actions, and relationships become more open, fulfilling, and responsive to each situation. The soul becomes increasingly patterned by Essence rather than by past conditioning. The unique individuality of our Being is more and more an expression of the pure qualities of Essence and not the counterfeit or compensatory qualities of the ego.

Yet as long as there is a sense of separate individual identity present in experience, ego patterns will block Being and maintain a sense, however subtle, of frustration and alienation. Essence by itself cannot completely replace or eliminate the ego's obscurations of our true nature. The qualities of Essence are not the whole story. As our understanding and experience of Essence deepens, other dimensions arise. The personal aspects of Essence fade out of awareness, and there is no longer a sense of individual identity or ego.

These dimensions are experienced without the bounds of a separate self. They are truly egoless. Without ego or a separate identity, there can be no duality between self and the self's true nature. Thus, they are also nondual. Because these dimensions are not limited by the patterns of past personal history or by the fixated structures of the ego, they are also boundless and formless. Ali has used all these terms: *egoless, nondual, formless, and boundless*. Each term adds an important nuance of understanding, although here I will refer to them usually as Boundless or nondual.

Because our usual experience is so heavily directed by the structures of the ego and because these dimensions are egoless, they are often difficult to grasp. Each of these dimensions has a sense of freedom, clarity, and reality that is unthinkable in ordinary experience. An ego-based frame of reference can only dimly glimpse such states, longing for them and struggling to gain such experiences. However, this struggle creates the shell around our experience that makes them less accessible. They are not something we can go after or achieve. The realization of boundlessness and nonduality happens only at levels beyond the ego and beyond all sense of effort. The Boundless dimensions of Being have their own principles. They are the deepest foundation of the Diamond Approach and all spiritual work and understanding.

Each of these dimensions has a set of psychological issues, resistances, and attachments that arise in conjunction with it. The source of these issues and misunderstandings is not the discrimination of dimensions of Being but *reification*. This term may not be familiar to you, but it is very helpful in understanding the obstacles to spiritual work. When we reify, we treat a quality, a process, or a flow as an object or a thing. Our concepts, beliefs, images, and representations about ourselves, others, and the world naturally arise and fall away in the flow of our soul. So do experiences of Essence. However, when we reify any of these, we make it seem like a fixed object that we can manipulate, push away, or hold on to. This is why reification is the basis of all attachments.

Attachments have a sense of anxiety, grasping, deficiency, and desperation about them. They make life seem heavy or frustrating. Reification is also the basis for misunderstandings and delusions about Being and true nature. To reify true nature makes it seem like something that we can gain or lose, something we have or lack.

The delusion that we lack intrinsic strength, for example, gives rise to a pattern of trying to increase what the ego thinks will make us strong. Experiencing the Strength Essence relieves this pattern in the ego. However, the Essential experience cannot completely penetrate or resolve the struggle to be strong. Even when we experience true strength as a quality of Essence, we still continue the search for it. As long as there is a separate identity, there will be a tendency to attach the quality of strength, or the sense of a lack of strength, to that identity. The perspective of the Boundless dimensions, however, is that strength is intrinsic to existence and therefore cannot be gained or lost. These dimensions allow our attachments and misconceptions about true nature to arise in order to be seen, understood, worked through, and integrated.

True Nature

It is helpful at this point to move toward a clearer definition of true nature as it is used in the Diamond Approach. I have used this term throughout this book, sometimes referring to true nature as objective reality or as Being. It is Being without any distortion by our personal history. The true nature of Being is not constructed or invented. We recognize it when we penetrate the subjective biases that obscure it. Then we see it without distortion and realize it is always here.

True nature gives a texture to our experiences. The more we are in touch with it, the more we find our experiences to be flowing, beautiful, full, clear, and pure. There is a sense of mystery. We become aware of the world, and our awareness is luminous, radiant, and delicate. We feel that everything is majestic and real. To the extent that we are in touch with true nature, all our experiences take on tones such as these. There is no particular experience or state that is "higher" or more valuable according to true nature. Instead, when we move deeply enough into any experience, it reveals its deepest characteristic and its true nature. True nature is not a state of consciousness; it is the ground of all consciousness.

There are many veils that separate us from an awareness of our true nature. In our usual experience, Essence and its specific aspects are veiled by ego. When we penetrate deeply enough into those veils, they dissolve, and the Essential aspects that were blocked are realized one by one. The true nature or ground of every ego-based experience is Essence. However, these personal, Essential aspects themselves can become veils. When that veil is parted, it reveals the true nature of Essence as boundless. Each dimension of boundlessness, in turn, is both a realization and a veil, until the absolute mystery is realized. The various Boundless dimensions of Being always coexist and are always present. At the same time, of course, we are usually asleep to them.

These boundless, egoless, and nondual dimensions have been recognized by various spiritual systems such as Dzogchen and Zen Buddhism, Kashmir Shaivism, mystical Christianity, Taoism, and Sufism, in addition to the Diamond Approach. These descriptions appear to be independent discoveries and not dependent on others' descriptions. Because they are remarkably similar, they do give credence to the existence and characteristics of true nature. At the same time, true nature lies beyond all descriptions and distinctions. The Diamond Approach goes beyond other descriptions of the nondual dimensions by showing the psychological issues and attachments that accompany each one. The understanding of the Diamond Approach also informs its methods and gives us precise and powerful ways of working with these issues.

Discriminating and describing these various dimensions of nonduality is often helpful for students if they are able to understand them in their own experience. At other times, it is more useful to see the true nature of Being as a unity that is beyond description and not to distinguish separate dimensions. The Diamond Approach is open to both perspectives and responsive to the specific needs of the student and the situation. Here I will briefly summarize the five Boundless dimensions in the hope that it will help make these deeper levels of experience more accessible to us.

DIVINE LOVE

The dimension of Boundless or Divine Love is often the first one encountered beyond the personal dimensions of Being. Through it, we experience the limitless richness and beauty of the world in an unconditionally loving way. Being reveals its nature as beauty and love. We discover we are always held in the arms of a limitless loving light or, as Ali calls it, the Living Daylight. It seems that all experiences and all forms are held in and pervaded by a universal and boundless loving embrace that is sweet, delicate, supportive, and unfailingly responsive to our deepest need. Experienced through the mental function, this dimension is a consciousness that is alive and radiant, revealing the beauty of existence. Experienced through the heart center or in a heartful way, it is more like a boundless love. Experienced through the belly center, Divine Love is felt as a conscious loving presence holding and enfolding us and the world.

Without the veils of dualistic identity, the world and all its constituents emerge in ever more exquisite ways, revealing their intrinsic glory and richness. Everything—including ego, suffering, attachment, and spirit—is seen as an expression and a manifestation of unconditional love. This is not a personal or an intellectual insight but rather a direct knowing of the nature of reality as love. When we go beyond the boundaries of the ego, the world does not disappear. Rather, we see it in its deeper characteristic, its loveliness, in a way that we could never perceive before.

THE SUPREME

Nondual consciousness does not stop with this beauty and love, despite our tendency to want to hold on to it and reside there. When this dimension of beauty and love is experienced deeply enough and without attachment, its nature is revealed as a fullness and presence. Beauty is now seen as a surface quality, and its substance or depth is pure existence. Within the lovingness of the world lies the fact of its presence. The world has a quality of presence, significance, profundity, and realness.

Only by transcending personal identity can this unbounded presence be experienced. The world is experienced as pure presence that is differentiated into universal noetic forms. This is the realm sometimes referred to as Gnosis or the nous. This dimension, corresponding to the "Universal Mind" or "Divine Mind," is the source of knowing because here knowing and being emerge as one phenomenon. Each experience discloses the prototypical concepts underlying it. (See Ali's reference to this dimension in the third excerpt in Chapter 2, from his book *Luminous Night's Journey*.)

For example, when I see a hawk soaring overhead, I see not only *this* particular hawk in *this* particular place. I also become aware of the noetic forms that underlie it. These may include the freedom of the hawk's flight, the clarity of its vision, and the integration of the effortless play of its wings on the westerly breeze with its single-minded devotion to finding a meal. In that moment, the hawk and I—indeed, the whole universe—are reflections on the same nonduality of relaxation and purpose. Then the hawk is gone, and other universal concepts come to the forefront of my awareness, giving rise to new experiences.

All is experienced as a unity, and at the same time, this unity is discriminated into knowable forms, such as hawk, wing, wind, relaxation, and purpose. The world and our experience are revealed as an exquisitely differentiated and luminous existence, palpable and precious. In this dimension, Being is existence and knowledge. Ali calls this differentiated unity the Supreme, referring to concepts of God or the universe as an all-inclusive and boundless presence.

The Nonconceptual

Penetrating the pure presence and unity of the world, we discover its ground as awareness with no content or concepts. We encounter the realm of nonconceptual awareness and emptiness, the ground of the Supreme. Here, we cannot say that reality is presence, since this dimension is beyond concepts, even the concept of presence. Thus, it has a quality of emptiness that is more fundamental than form. It can have no name because any name would fix it and make it into a concept. Thus, Ali also calls it the Nameless.

Although empty of concepts, this dimension has a sense of newness and freshness to it. In fact, *because* it is empty of concepts, it is continuously fresh and new. The true nature of the world is fully transparent. Our perception has a quality of bare awareness without concepts or labels. We perceive the world, but it is as if each perception were brand-new and undistorted by our memories and expectations. Any reification or fixing of any aspect of experience blocks this dimension. Therefore, the pure awareness of the Nameless is nonconceptual. This makes for a paradoxical, koanlike exercise in talking about that which cannot be talked about. As soon as we say anything about this dimension, we are out of it. It can only be known without concepts, and any recognition or perception of it, other than a pure, bare awareness, is not it. There is only a mirrorlike perception without commentary, reaction, or even knowing. Now, Being is a completely clear, crystalline, light, and spacious quality. It is a luminous emptiness, reflecting the true nature beyond concepts and existence.

THE LOGOS

In the Logos, the world is experienced as a pure, flowing, dynamic unfoldment in each moment. This dimension coexists with all the other Boundless dimensions. The experience of Divine Love, the Supreme, and even the experience of the Nonconceptual dimension all have a quality of change. None of the Boundless dimensions described so far can account for this transitory quality. The Logos is Being as dynamic flow. It is the fact that the world is born anew each moment. This dynamism reveals the world's aliveness and its continual unfoldment and flowering.

From this dimension, the world is seen in its eternal and timeless unfoldment and change. The world is revealed as a dance, always moving. Yet this movement is not haphazard but organized. All of our sensations, thoughts, feelings, all of the continual moment-to-moment changes in the physical world, and paradoxically, even the Supreme unity and the Nameless emptiness are an unfoldment of this dynamism and flow.

The Logos is also referred to as the "Universal Soul," the soul of the universe. It is similar to the personal soul or the individual consciousness that experiences except that it is boundless and egoless. Being is a constant movement of creation and renewal, and when there are no personal barriers or fixations to that renewal, it is a revelation. Constantly revealing itself, Being is manifesting all the qualities of its true nature simultaneously.

Being is constantly articulating itself, which is recognized by calling this dimension the Logos. Logos refers to the "original Word" or the harmonious and organized unfoldment of Being. This Word is the initial, original form or pattern of Being and the basis for our knowing and communicating about Being. Thus, in the Logos, our knowing of Being, its expression, and its flow arise together. It is the Story behind all stories, the Voice before all voices.

THE ABSOLUTE

Ali describes a deeper reality fundamental to each of these, a fifth Boundless dimension. He calls this the Absolute. It is a dimension beyond change, richness, beauty, fullness, or emptiness. The Absolute is the unknowable origin and ultimate nature of Being. At this level, all paradoxes dissolve, including the paradox that existence is both full and empty, present and absent. The Absolute is beyond all qualities of Being, including awareness, consciousness, and knowing. At the beginning, it is experienced only as a cessation and an absence. There is no perception, no awareness that there is no perception, and no movement. We can compare it to the state of consciousness in deep sleep or the state of the universe before the big bang. It is an ultimate, unconditional, and imperturbable peace.

Yet this peace is not an end. The Absolute begins to unfold with a preciousness and luminosity that are beyond words. We come to realize that everything is always the Absolute—all forms, appearances, birth, death, emptiness, and fullness.

The Absolute brings the understanding that everything we experience is only the surface, with the Absolute as the back or the inside of this surface. It is that which cannot be known, an ultimate mystery. Everything we see is a thin bubble over this complete mystery. All of creation arises from this mysterious ground and is therefore never separate from it. This is the source of the experience of complete liberation and complete nonduality. Although it is its nature to be indescribable and unknowable, a number of spiritual teachers and traditions have touched this mystery and recognized it as the source of freedom and liberation. Ali's book *Luminous Night's Journey* includes accounts of this dimension, and it is integrated into the later parts of his books *The Void, The Pearl beyond Price,* and *The Point of Existence.*

The Journeys of Ascent and Descent

I have presented these descriptions of the Boundless dimensions of Being in a somewhat linear way according to what is often called the journey of ascent. This is the usual experience of the development of consciousness from the perspective of the individual. This journey is focused on the soul and its development, maturation, and refinement. As it develops, it reveals increasingly deeper levels, each disclosing its true nature, all the way to the absolute mystery as the true nature and ultimate ground of all.

Similarly, Being unfolds and manifests in an orderly way from the absolute mystery into the multitude of forms and objects of the phenomenal world. As is unfolds, it flows through these various dimensions in a progression from those closer to the mystery to those closer to the phenomenal world, a so-called journey of descent.

In the view of the Diamond Approach, both of these journeys and all of these dimensions are always present, coexisting and coemerging. These dimensions are complementary and equally valid. Immanence, fullness, and the myriad forms of the world are one side of a coin; transcendence, emptiness, and the mystery of union are the other. Thus, the richness and beauty of the world are no more true, valuable, or privileged than its emptiness. Absence and fullness are equally real, as are beauty and flow. All are manifestations of the same ground of Being and its true nature.

I would note that in none of these descriptions is there a sense of *leaving* the world, only of seeing it more deeply or clearly. This is summarized by the spiritual aphorism at the heart of the Diamond Approach, "to be in the world but not of it."

In the following selections, Ali gives brief descriptions of the five Boundless dimensions. Universal Love is another name for Divine Love, Pure Being is the Supreme, Nonconceptual Reality is the Nameless, and Absolute Truth is another term for what he has called simply the Absolute. These four selections are from *The Point of Existence*, Ali's book on the true identity and its relation to narcissism. Because of this, they are set in the context of his discussion of narcissism, the ego-shell, and the self. The selection on the Logos is from *The Pearl beyond Price*. In both of these books, Ali points to parallels and similarities with other spiritual systems. These selections appear near the end of these two books. He offers these descriptions only after more than three hundred pages of careful analysis and groundwork. Ali's discussions of the Boundless dimensions here, as well as in *Diamond Heart, Book 4,* and *Luminous Night's Journey,* are very advanced. Once again, I refer interested readers to the original books by Ali for a fuller discussion of this material.

Divine Love

As we explore the barriers to self-realization, we need to inquire into our basic distrust. This will take us into exploring our early holding environment and its effects on the development of our sense of self. Investigating the inadequacies of our early holding environment reveals the effects of these inadequacies on our particular self-identity structure. Working through this history, and illuminating the psychic structures it has created, leads finally to the awareness of the absence of basic holding. This absence is associated with a certain emptiness, the hole of a specific manifestation of Being. Learning to allow this emptiness finally ushers us into this manifestation of Being, which turns out to be a quality of love. It is a quality of boundless and gentle love, a delicate light experienced as the presence of softness, sweetness and generosity. It is not exactly a personal kind of love. It is love for everything and everyone—universal love.

Its direct effect on the self is for her to feel lovingly held, as if cuddled in the infinitely loving arms of the universe. It also brings the perception that this loving, holding quality is intrinsic to the fundamental ground of all existence. The more she experiences this loving manifestation of Being, the more her basic trust develops, and the more her faith in reality is restored.

The issues of basic trust and the surrender that it engenders are not specific to the work on narcissism. However, some resolution of these issues is necessary for the surrender involved in slowing down and ceasing ego activity. The realization of this quality of love, which we call Living Daylight or Loving Light, resolves these issues. The presence of the Living Daylight helps us to let go of the empty shell, to allow the narcissistic wound and accept the narcissistic emptiness. This boundless, loving presence makes it easier for the self to relax and cease activity. We also come to understand that it is this love which actually acts, and not the self. It is the melting action of this love that finally dissolves the ego activity.

Pure Being and the Supreme

Recognizing that Being is actually infinite and not bounded by any partitions has profound implications. One important one is that Being is the ground of everything and everyone. In other words, there is only one indivisible Being which is the nature and Essence of everything.

Here, we know ourselves as a presence totally pure and completely real. It is so pure it has no qualities; it is just the fact of beingness experienced as an ontological presence. This presence is clarity, lightness, transparency, all ineffable and precious in an undefinable way. It is so ineffable that it feels both empty and full simultaneously. There is the sense of being wide awake, with fresh awareness and lucid perception.

In this manifestation of Being, we know Being in its purity, before differentiation and discrimination, before labeling and reaction. There are no differentiated qualities, but nothing is missing. We experience a completeness. It is as if all the qualities are present before differentiation. Before this discovery, our experience of Being takes the form of one of its differentiated manifestations—like love, intelligence, or even identity—but now we know ourselves purely, before recognizable and conceptualizable qualities.

The other important discovery we make at this point is that Being is inherently boundless. We experience this purity of presence as pervasive and infinite, and see, also, that it underlies everything. We come to see that pure Being is the essence and true nature of all manifestation, not only of the self. Further, we experience Being not only as the essence of everything, but as everything. It constitutes not only the core of everything, but the very substance and fabric of everything. It is a medium inside every object, outside it, and in between the outside and inside. It makes up the very substance of the form, not only what fills it. It is both the essence and the boundaries of all forms. So Being is the nature, essence, and substance of all physical objects, all mental objects, and all experienceable manifestations. It is the body, the feelings, the thoughts, the actions, the sounds, the sights, and the meanings. Being is everything.

At this level of realization, we come also to perceive the unity of all manifestation. Since Being is an indivisible medium (not composed of parts), it follows that everything makes up a unity, a oneness. There is one existence, as opposed to two, or many. It is merely an infinite presence that possesses a pattern. This pattern is everything we perceive, including all persons and objects. So everything is connected to everything; there exist no separate and autonomous objects or persons.

Nonconceptual Reality and the Nameless

[Seeing how we have reified even the oneness] precipitates the movement of our identity into a subtler manifestation of Being, a totally nonconceptual realization of true nature. We experience ourselves now as nonconceptual reality, beyond all mind and concepts, beyond all specifications and recognitions. We cannot even say whether we are being or nonbeing, absence or presence. Existence is negated, and this negation in turn is negated. Our recognition of ourselves negates both negation and affirmation of any attributes, which is a much more profound experience of Being than that of pure Being [the Supreme]. There is now no definite sense of any concept, reality, thing, or manifestation. We are both existence and nonexistence, not existence and not nonexistence. We are both self and not self. This is a very paradoxical manifestation of Being, beyond any conceptualization.

This experience is boundless, but it does not feel as clear as presence or fullness. It is like experiencing the inside of all of the universe as a totally clear and completely transparent, crystalline medium. There is no iota of obscuration or impediment, just an infinity of transparent clarity. There is a stunning sense of awakeness, intensely fresh and new. When there are no concepts in our recognition of ourselves, nothing is old; everything is the pure freshness of suchness, the intensity of eternity that has no concept of time.

The recognition of ourselves has no mental elaboration; it is the totally pure being of transparent crystalline clarity. There is a solidity of presence, an infinite immensity that feels at the same time absolutely empty and nonexistent. We know our nature as the most solid and fundamental ground of all appearance, without this nature taking on any sense of fullness or substance. It is a totally solid, complete absence, which shatters the mind with its cool transparency.

In this manifestation there is no sense of individual or self, but no sense of their absence, for either would be a concept. Everything seems to be part of this immense clarity, which is totally itself, without it needing to be conceptualized. All objects and persons appear as part of this transparent clarity, pervaded with it, constituted of it, but only as transparent patterns in this nameless reality. Thus, duality is transcended before it is even conceptualized.

The only thing that is there is consciousness. But consciousness here is not exactly a concept; it is just the fact of consciousness. We are not unconscious, that's all. There is consciousness, but there is no one who is conscious. Here, we are going into the true nature of Being, the true nature of God, or the true nature of the universe, before any mind, before any conceptualization, before any specification, before any differentiation, before we can experience or say anything; so this pure consciousness is beyond experience, beyond mind, beyond concept, beyond all these things.

This nonconceptual awareness is truly radical. While it does not affirm any concept, neither does it negate or deny any concept. To negate is to affirm and to affirm is to negate, for in both cases a concept is present. This reality is prior to any concept, and hence, possesses no presupposition whatsoever. Purity of Being is now nonconceptual, so it is complete, and recognized as the fundamental reality of all experience.

The Logos

[The Logos] is one of the Boundless dimensions, quite distinct from the other dimensions we have discussed so far, which are all experienced as the presence of Being. They are different manifestations of Being, where Being is a stillness, an existence, a thereness, a presence. There is no movement of Being here, or functioning.

The Diamond Approach

The Logos, on the other hand, is the presence of Being in a boundless manifestation that has a distinct dynamic quality to it. It is experienced as Being in flow, in movement. The flow and movement are not haphazard, but coincide with the changes we see as the occurrence of events in the totality of the whole universe. In other words, all changes are perceived from this dimension as the flow of substance and beingness of the Logos. The world is perceived, in some sense, as alive and living, as one infinite and boundless organism of consciousness. It is not merely the presence of Being or consciousness; this dimension of Being is experienced as a living organism, boundless and infinite.

Movements, changes and transformations in the universe are then perceived as the functioning of this dimension. The whole universe is perceived to move, change and transform as a unity. This is universal or cosmic functioning, not related to a distinct entity in the world. This is admittedly rather mysterious, even unbelievable, when not experienced directly. It is the basis for the Western prophetic tradition's concept of a God that creates and runs the universe. The Sufis associate this dimension, the Logos, with the prophet of Islam, Mohammed, just as Christianity associates it with the Christ.

The flow of the beingness of the Logos is seen as cosmic functioning. It is the same as the process of continual creation, which is a manifestation of all existence from the Absolute. This kind of functioning can be perceived or experienced in different ways, depending on what Boundless dimension we are perceiving this flow from. Any rigidity in the personality, which is an expression of the ego's need for a lasting and unchanging structure, becomes a psychodynamic issue at this level.

The dimension of the Logos is integrative in nature, and can be experienced as the totality of all dimensions, except for the Absolute. Hence, it is often seen as the totality of existence, termed sometimes "creation." It is difficult to explain what this means, but it must suffice to state that the Logos brings about the capacity to see that all aspects and dimensions of Being can be perceived as one, as the manifest part of the Truth, contrasted to the Absolute which is the unmanifest Truth.

The Absolute

If we are not bound by our habitual beliefs, we might come to realize that we long to disappear, to gently vanish, to be no more. We experience a very deep weariness, and a teary subtle longing, that sometimes becomes powerful and passionate, to simply fade away, and not to leave any trace. We find the notion of absolute cessation sweet and dear to our heart. We feel that not to be, not even to know that we are not, would be the final release from a life of striving and searching. We contemplate not being as some kind of ultimate, albeit obscure, fulfillment of our heart. It is as if we sense that only not being will bring contentment, and a peace beyond peace.

This gentle disappearing will actually come to pass if the process takes its course. We will have the experience once in a while—especially when we are relaxed and mentally uncon-cerned—of feeling our selves disappearing. There will be a gap in consciousness, a cessation of all sensation and perception, without falling asleep or unconscious. We know this because, when we come to, we feel quite rested but also indescribably clear and fresh, as if our soul has been washed of its heaviness and conflicts. We feel lucid and totally carefree, light and totally lighthearted. No sleep ever rejuvenates us this much. It is as if not only our bodies, but our very selves and souls have been renewed. We do not remember what happened because abso-lutely nothing has happened. There was absolutely no content of experience.

This is the beginning of tasting the absolute depth of our Being, although the encounter is still limited. We still need to understand and let go of the subtle vestiges of representations. This transpires in many ways. One of the most significant ways is to follow the narcissistic emptiness related to the approaching depth of Being. We feel empty and impoverished. If we manage not to reject, judge, or react to this emptiness, we begin to realize how impoverished we actually are. We feel devoid of significance or value, of Essence or substance; we feel that we have only attachments. We begin to feel that we have to let go of everything because we do not possess anything. We have to let go of our attachment to relationships, pleasure, comfort, security, knowledge, Essence, realization, enlightenment, ego, self, suffering, and so on. Holding on to any of these attachments simply means resisting awareness of the poverty of the denuded shell of the self. We realize we need to let go of having—or let go of the belief that we have—a position, a place, recognition, fruit of work, accomplishment, contribution, knowledge, even state or development. We need to let go of everything if we are not going to spend the rest of our lives fighting the emptiness of our shell. This activates deep grief, very deep sadness and tears. The emptiness becomes a vast black ocean of tears.

We realize that in identifying with the ego-self we truly have nothing, for everything comes from Being. As the ego-self, we are fundamentally poor, totally indigent, devoid of all possessions and qualities. This state is very profound; by this point, too, we are coming to the insight that this is the intrinsic condition of the ego-self, and is not particular only to our personal situation. The state has a sense of having nothing, feeling nothing, being nothing, and perceiving nothing. It can easily shift to the state of cessation (the disappearing), but it can go further.

This state of poverty, which some traditions call "mystical poverty," is the expression of the transformation of narcissistic emptiness into true inner spaciousness, a profound void now penetrating the shell due to the shell's almost complete denudement. As the self is letting go of its representations of itself, which feels like the surrendering of everything we believed we possessed, we become increasingly transparent to the presentations of Being. We experience a new profundity of true emptiness—black space—but it is reflected through a slight vestige of

♦

THE FLAME OF THE SEARCH, GUIDANCE, AND THE LOVE OF TRUTH

T HIS BOOK STARTED on a personal note. Then it described and illustrated the main concepts and methods of the Diamond Approach. Now it is time to direct it to you and your journey. Your immediate experience—approached with courage, compassion, trust, and surrender—is both the path and the fulfillment of your potential as a human being. Living fully and openly is possible. This is the promise of the Diamond Approach.

However, this promise is not fulfilled automatically or even easily. Sincere commitment and dedicated practice are required. Three specific capacities will serve you in the work of realizing and developing your potential. These are not the only three, of course, but they are helpful, even necessary, at all stages of spiritual work.

First, there is the inner fire that motivates and fuels this work. Ali calls this the flame of the search. At first, it may feel like an itch in your soul or a longing that returns again and again. Your suffering may wake you up to this fire. It can start as an ember that, when touched by the breath of your sincerity, catches fire, calling you out of your sleep, calling you to look deeply into yourself. All the layers of veils that have built up through your life make the work unbelievably arduous. And it is exactly here that the flame serves you, bringing the energy it takes to stay with your journey.

What is motivating your questions and your search right now? What keeps you asking for a more meaningful and fulfilling life? Can you recognize the flame in yourself as a kind of hunger, a desire, a longing? The feeling may be subtle at first, but it will grow. If you can let this flame get stronger, it will burn away your dullness, your preconceptions, your judgments, your stuckness. It will bring you into contact with yourself in a stark and relentless way. I encourage you to let this burning itself become the goal—not feeling better, not learning, not achieving, but simply being on fire with your search.

Now, when you let down the armor of your beliefs, you will find you really don't know what you need or where you need to go. You'll discover that every intention and every direction you can think to go is a product of your conditioning. Every aim, no matter how lofty it seems, comes from a hole, a feeling of deficiency. When you use this flame to enter that hole, you open yourself to unthinkable new possibilities, unthinkable because your past history made them so.

This flame burns even brighter when you allow yourself to not know. Then, another capacity arises—a guidance. At first, your ego says, "Oh, good, now I'll get a direction." Yet the guidance does not give you a direction, at least not the kind your ego recognizes. This guidance brings you deeper into the present and helps you drop the prejudices of your past. It directs you to question all those old stories you've been telling yourself for years, the stories about your weakness, your wrongness, your separateness, or your deficiency. When you drop your pseudoknowing, you enter a kind of emptiness or ignorance.

What would it mean to open yourself to not knowing

where you are going or what you need? Could you, right now, suspend your plans and ideas about where to go next, for just a moment? Can you trust the guidance—or at least begin to see what blocks you from trusting it? (Revealing the obstacles is the action of guidance, too.) How would it be if you were to bow to the guidance, even if it brings up fear or hurt? In bowing to it, you honor its wisdom. Then, you sit up straight again, willing to follow the guidance for at least one more step. The guidance will always lead you toward what matters, toward greater presence. Ali writes:

> Begin with the awareness that you don't know the answers. And be aware of the feverish attempts in your mind to convince yourself that you know. It's not only that you don't know the answers, you don't know whether the questions can be answered. Allow the questions to remain even if you don't know whether there is an answer. Can you be that sincere with yourself? There is guidance and help here, but not to give answers, only to help you inquire. This Work is to encourage your own inner development, whatever that may be, to help you remain steadfast with your inquiry. (*Diamond Heart, Book 3*, p. 4)

There is a third capacity along with the flame of the search and the guidance that this work requires. In some sense, it is the most fundamental. It is the love of truth. When you love the truth, you love it unconditionally, not because it will make you feel better and not because it will make you free. The love itself is the freedom.

The guidance will lead you to this love, and the flame will energize your search, but only if you are willing to give yourself to the work. You don't have to do this all at once, but just turning toward this love will carry you on. Turn yourself toward loving just what is. Turn yourself toward the pain that leads you to the flame and toward the emptiness that opens you to the guidance. Compassion befriends you as you sit with your pain, and a playful curiosity reassures you with its lightness. Turning toward the love of truth will empower you to give yourself more fully to your journey. Love is the key to giving yourself in this way.

The beauty of the Diamond Approach is that it helps you understand the need to love the truth, the barriers to this love, and the connection between love and its obstacles. If loving the truth, surrendering to the guidance, or fueling your flame were merely spiritual commands, they would be virtually impossible. Look how many people have been exposed to such teachings and how few have been able to realize them in their lives. As I have tried to show, the Diamond Approach illuminates the barriers to spiritual work as well as its possibilities. You can know that these challenges bring with them whatever you need in order to solve them. You can understand how the key to your freedom lies within—not outside—your prison. As you look into your experience in the present moment, you will begin to see what's in your way. And when you see, the obstacle begins to transform.

When I talk about the need to surrender, your unconscious may begin to recall times as a child when you were in a conflict and were hurt. Maybe you remember times when you didn't know something and you were shamed for not knowing "the answer" or for not meeting someone else's standards. You may have learned to give yourself away, but only as an attempt to avoid aloneness and to get by in your family. Or you may find yourself having some reactions to what I have said about the Diamond Approach. You may feel angered, scared, or saddened by these descriptions. You may feel it is too obtuse, judgmental, or out of touch with reality. It is helpful to recognize these reactions and allow yourself to look into them and their roots.

If you look deeply into your experience, you will find exactly, precisely, 100 percent what you need to continue your inquiry. Through your hurt, you will find the compassion to tolerate the hurt and go deeper. Through your shame, you will come to the sense of dignity that allows you to open more. Through your fear of aloneness, you will discover the support you need to persevere with confidence. In your reactivity, you may find that you have projected your past hurts into the present, and through it, you will come to an unshakable acceptance of your life. All the qualities and dimensions of Essence are available to you to further your inquiry into the truth.

As you let the flame fuel your search, as you let your not-knowing make room for the guidance to come in, and as you begin to love the truth unconditionally, your life unfolds with power, tenderness, and meaning. Ali, again:

> When you really get into seeing things about yourself, it's very painful. You don't like it, but something in you says, "I want to feel this and get to the bottom of it." Nobody's making you do it. So in that moment, what is compelling you? It is somehow your desire to see the truth. Seeing the truth seems to be fulfilling in itself, it seems to bring some subtle pleasure and joy. So you want to see it regardless of how difficult it is. It is no longer a question of what is a true statement or perception or not. There is something more, and something more subtle. It is, in a sense, that the truth wants itself. And that's what is called the love of truth for its own sake. In that situation, it is such a deep, compelling desire that when it is there, nothing can stand in its way—not fear, not pain. (*Diamond Heart, Book 1,* pp. 96–97)

Finally, you come to the deepest realization, which is the source of the flame, the guidance, and the love of truth. You see that all along it has been the truth of Being seeking itself. Being is aware of itself through you. Your mind, your search, your joy, your love, your emptiness, and the unfathomable mystery of your existence—these are its organs of perception.

Then you discover that the fulfillment of your life is serving Being. Your life is an expression of Being, and the highest action you can take is to give yourself to Being. When you serve Being fully, you dedicate yourself to awakening your senses so that Being perceives itself more fully. You work to purify and clarify your soul so that the Absolute flows through it with grace and ease. You open your heart to both give it away and receive the Divine. You welcome your joy, because this way Being knows its joy. Your knowledge and understanding are the ways Being knows and understands itself. Your life becomes a vehicle for Being.

To be sure, there is much hard work to be done. But the next step is always just in front of you. Each moment you have the opportunity to open yourself to Being. Each time you are even a little bit more aware of your breath and the world around you, Being comes closer to itself, and your life is infused with a touch of contentment. When you are open to your particular suffering and willing to be empty, alone, and intimate with yourself, your true nature is revealed. Being comes to know its own Essence.

You don't have to do it all at once, just the next little bit. I invite you to turn toward the presence of your life as it is right now, in this moment.

◆

BIBLIOGRAPHY

ALI HAS AUTHORED TWO SERIES of books: the Diamond Heart Series and the Diamond Mind Series. The Diamond Heart books (1 through 4, with more planned) are transcripts of talks given to students in a spiritual group directed by Ali. The material covered in the Diamond Heart books progresses as the students learned. The Diamond Mind books are written for a professional audience interested in a thorough treatment of theoretical and technical issues in the Diamond Approach. The following books, listed in chronological order within each group, were all authored by A. H. Almaas (Ali's pen name):

The Elixir of Enlightenment. York Beach, Maine: Samuel Weiser, 1984.
Essence: The Diamond Approach to Inner Realization. York Beach, Maine: Samuel Weiser, 1986.
Facets of Unity: The Enneagram of Holy Ideas. Berkeley, Calif.: Diamond Books, 1998.

THE DIAMOND HEART SERIES

Diamond Heart, Book 1: Elements of the Real in Man. Berkeley, Calif.: Diamond Books, 1987.
Diamond Heart, Book 2: The Freedom to Be. Berkeley, Calif.: Diamond Books, 1988.
Diamond Heart, Book 3: Being and the Meaning of Life. Berkeley, Calif.: Diamond Books, 1990.

Diamond Heart, Book 4: Indestructible Innocence. Berkeley, Calif.: Diamond Books, 1997.

THE DIAMOND MIND SERIES

The Void: A Psychodynamic Investigation of the Relationship between Mind and Space. Berkeley, Calif.: Diamond Books, 1986.

The Pearl beyond Price: Integration of Personality into Being: An Object Relations Approach. Berkeley, Calif.: Diamond Books, 1988.

The Point of Existence: Transformations of Narcissism in Self-Realization. Berkeley, Calif.: Diamond Books, 1996.

Interested readers can obtain a catalogue of many of Almaas's books from:

Diamond Books
P.O. Box 10114
Berkeley, CA 94709–5114
USA

The following books are based on the Diamond Approach, discuss its influence, or include chapters by Almaas:

Binet, Calla Marie. *Tears Flow, Ice Melts, Spring Comes!: A Soul Blossoms.* P.O. Box 20815, Boulder, Colo.: Golden Reed, 1997.

Brown, Byron. *Soul without Shame: A Guide to Liberating Yourself from the Judge Within.* Boston: Shambhala Publications, 1998.

Carlson, Richard, and Benjamin Shield, eds. *For the Love of God: New Writings by Spiritual and Psychological Leaders.* Novato, Calif.: New World Library, 1990.

Cortright, Brant. *Psychotherapy and Spirit: Theory and Practice in Transpersonal Psychotherapy.* Albany: State University of New York Press, 1997.

Kornfield, Jack. *A Path with Heart: A Guide through the Perils and Promises of Spiritual Life.* New York: Bantam Books, 1993.

Roth, Geneen. *Appetites: On the Search for True Nourishment.* New York: Dutton, 1996.

Schwartz, Tony. *What Really Matters: Searching for Wisdom in America.* New York: Bantam Books, 1995.

Welwood, John, ed. *Ordinary Magic: Everyday Life as Spiritual Path.* Boston: Shambhala Publications, 1992.

Wilber, Ken. *The Eye of Spirit: An Integral Vision for a World Gone Slightly Mad.* Boston: Shambhala Publications, 1997.

The Ridhwan Foundation maintains a World Wide Web site with information on the Diamond Approach, books by Almaas, and ways to study this work.

Ridhwan Foundation: <http://www.ridhwan.org/dappr.html>

The Diamond Approach is taught by teachers trained and certified by the Ridhwan Foundation. For information on studying the Diamond Approach, write:

Ridhwan
P.O. Box 10114
Berkeley, CA 94709-5114
USA

♦

SOURCES AND CREDITS

WITH THANKS TO THE FOLLOWING publishers for granting permission to use portions of the material in this book:

Diamond Books (Box 10114, Berkeley, Calif. 94709), for excerpts from the following books by A. H. Almaas:

> The Void: A Psychodynamic Investigation of the Relationship between Mind and Space (1986)
> Diamond Heart, Book 1: Elements of the Real in Man (1987)
> Diamond Heart, Book 2: The Freedom to Be (1988)
> The Pearl beyond Price: Integration of Personality into Being: An Object Relations Approach (1988)
> Diamond Heart, Book 3: Being and the Meaning of Life (1990)
> Luminous Night's Journey: An Autobiographical Fragment (1995)
> The Point of Existence: Transformations of Narcissism in Self-Realization (1996)
> Used by permission.

Samuel Weiser (Box 612, York Beach, Maine 03910), for excerpts from the following books by A. H. Almaas:

> The Elixir of Enlightenment (1984). Used by permission.
> Essence: The Diamond Approach to Inner Realization (1986). Used by permission.

The following excerpts have been reprinted in this book:

CHAPTER 8. SELF-REALIZATION AND ESSENTIAL IDENTITY: THE POINT

CHAPTER 9. TRUE NATURE AND THE BOUNDLESS DIMENSIONS

◆

ACKNOWLEDGMENTS

WHEN I WAS CONSIDERING turning my short manuscript into a book introducing the Diamond Approach, I spoke with Sara Hurley, manager of Diamond Books. She put me in touch with Emily Hilburn Sell at Shambhala Publications. It was Emily's vision that brought together the combination of my overviews with selections from Hameed's writings. I am grateful to both Sara and Emily for their foresight about what this book could be. Sara's enthusiasm supported this project through its many stages. Emily's skill and good will were essential, too.

I also gratefully acknowledge the assistance of several people who helped edit early drafts of this book, especially Jasmin Cori. She made helpful suggestions about the overall organization, painstakingly reviewed the writing itself, and asked good, hard questions. Bob Rosenbush, Alia Johnson, Bob Ball, Linda Krier, Rennie Moran, Deane Shank, Byron Brown, Skip Ackler, Kirk Dennis, and others read parts of the manuscript and gave me valuable and helpful feedback. Sharon Binder, Scott Layton, Duncan Scribner, Mary Plumb, and others made helpful contributions. Nancy Jane and Mary McHenry provided important, fresh perspectives and useful suggestions, and I thank them.

Thanks to my friends, colleagues, and teachers who are helping me understand myself and this world.

My students, both within the Ridhwan School and in my college classes, have been and continue to be important teachers to me. This book owes a great deal to the students who read early rough drafts of this material and patiently let me know what worked and what didn't.

I am especially and enormously grateful to my family. Judith read parts of this manuscript at many different stages, and her encouragement and feedback helped to shape it. She also gave me much-needed support at crucial times in the process of writing. I bow to honor her inspiration and passion for life. Here's to my children, Geoffrey, Caroline, and Lucian. May their futures be bright, challenging, and fruitful.

The Metropolitan State College of Denver provided me several professional development grants, which allowed me time away from my teaching duties in order to work on parts of this book. I appreciate the support of my department chairwoman, Lyn Wickelgren, and my dean, Joan Foster.

My greatest debt and gratitude go to Hameed Ali. Over the twenty-four years he has been my teacher, I have come to know his love and compassion, his startling and brilliant capacity for understanding, and his unceasing allegiance to the truth. Without my contact with him and without his teaching, I would not have been able to write this book. First, I do not believe I would have discovered this knowledge myself. Although this book expresses my own understanding and style, Hameed's teaching has led me to it. Second, I am not sure I would have been able to sustain the perseverance, confidence, will, clarity, focus, humility, and openness necessary to write it without the teaching and guidance he has given me. It is my privilege to offer this book to him and to the Diamond Approach.

John Davis
Longmont, Colorado
June 2, 1998

INDEX

Spiritual transformation, 116, 121–22
Spiritual work. *See* Soul, work; Work
Spirituality, 55; and Personalness, 116–21
Splitting, 96, 97
Strength, 29–30, 85–86, 95, 97, 115; loss of, 105
Strength Essence. *See* Essential Strength
Subject-object dichotomy, 140–41
Suffering, 17–18, 20, 21, 33, 89, 91, 92, 96
Sunyata, 68
Superego, 28–29
Support *vs.* nonsupport, 96
Supreme, the, 149–51, 155–57
Supreme aspects, 109
Surrender, 20, 102, 166
Swamp Thing, 53–60

Teachers, Diamond Approach, 28, 52, 63, 102; and groups, 31–32
Teaching, 32, 108–10
Theory of Holes, 95, 96, 100–108. *See also* Holes
Time, passage of, 40
Timelessness, 40
Transformation, spiritual, 116, 121–22
Transpersonal psychology, 111
Trauma, 103, 104

True identity, 52
True nature, 7, 11, 12, 22, 35, 53, 54, 75, 83, 88, 105, 106, 116, 118, 134, 150, 158; of Being and Essence, 147; definition, 146–47; experience of, 25; identification with our, 131. *See also* Essence; Essential nature
Trungpa, Chögyam, 81
Truth, love of, 165–66. *See also* Absolute

Understanding, 8, 23–26, 75; Being and, 32–36; of immediate experience, 7
Unfoldment, 13–14, 50
Unity, 150, 151; non-differentiated state of, 103

Value, 101
The Void, 63, 68, 153

Will, 19–20, 22–23, 30, 96, 113, 116, 134; blocking and repression of, 19–20, 105; false, 97
Wisdom, spiritual, 9, 10, 128, 129; integration of psychodynamic psychology and, 129–30
Work, the, 105, 112, 165; Diamond Approach to, 17–23; Essence and, 89, 102; goal/purpose, 18, 101. *See also* Psychological work; Soul, work